U.S.S. Monitor National Marine Sanctuary

Management Plan

February 1983

U.S. DEPARTMENT OF COMMERCE
National Oceanic and Atmospheric Administration
Office of Ocean and Coastal Resource Management
Washington, D.C.

North Carolina
Department of Cultural Resources
Raleigh, N.C.

This document is a revised edition of the 1982 MONITOR National Marine Sanctuary Management Plan. This plan will be reviewed and updated annually by NOAA with assistance from North Carolina's Division of Archives and History, the MONITOR Technical Advisory Committee, and the MONITOR Federal Review Committee. NOAA welcomes your comments on this plan by October 1, 1983 for consideration during preparation of the 1984 plan.

TABLE OF CONTENTS

SUMMARY

On March 9, 1862, at Hampton Roads, Virginia, the USS MONITOR fought what has become the most celebrated battle in American naval history. This historic engagement, the first battle of ironclad warships, was the highlight of a promising service career cut short when the "Cheese-box-on-a-raft" was lost at sea on December 31, 1862. While the MONITOR proved to be as "impregnable" to shot and shell as the designer, Swedish-American engineer John Ericsson, had promised, the ironclad was unable to weather heavy gale-driven seas off Cape Hatteras, North Carolina.

1

Eleven months after being launched at Greenpoint, Long Island, the U.S.S. MONITOR and sixteen members of the crew disappeared in the "Graveyard of the Atlantic."

In 1973, an interdisciplinary scientific party employed intensive historical research and sophisticated electronic equipment to locate and subsequently identify the historic warship's remains. Announcement of the discovery stimulated considerable interest in further investigation of the wreck, recovery of artifacts associated with the ship, and possible salvage of the remains of the vessel. To ensure that the MONITOR would be preserved for systematic scientific investigation and development as a resource of national significance, the wreck was designated as the United States first national marine sanctuary by the U.S. Department of Commerce on January 30, 1975.

Duke University vessel EASTWARD, designated specifically for marine biological and geological investigation, served as the research platform for the 1973 expedition that located the remains of the MONITOR.

U.S.S. MONITOR (Painting by Alan Chesley)

Today the remains of John Ericsson's "Cheesebox-on-a-Raft" represent a unique legacy from the past. The shipwreck and its contents preserve an irreplaceable historical record and represent a monument to the American naval tradition the MONITOR helped to create.

John Ericsson

Officers examine the turret following the MONITOR's historic engagement at Hampton Roads. Dents in the turret were inflicted by the VIRGINIA during the 4 hour battle. (Courtesy of National Archives)

An indication of the historical data and cultural material protected at the MONITOR National Marine Sanctuary is apparent in the few existing photographs of the warship. (Courtesy of National Archives)

Diver working within the grid frame during archaeological site testing conducted in 1979. Artist's sketch (below) of diver and submersible JOHNSON SEA LINK. (Sketch by Joan Jannaman)

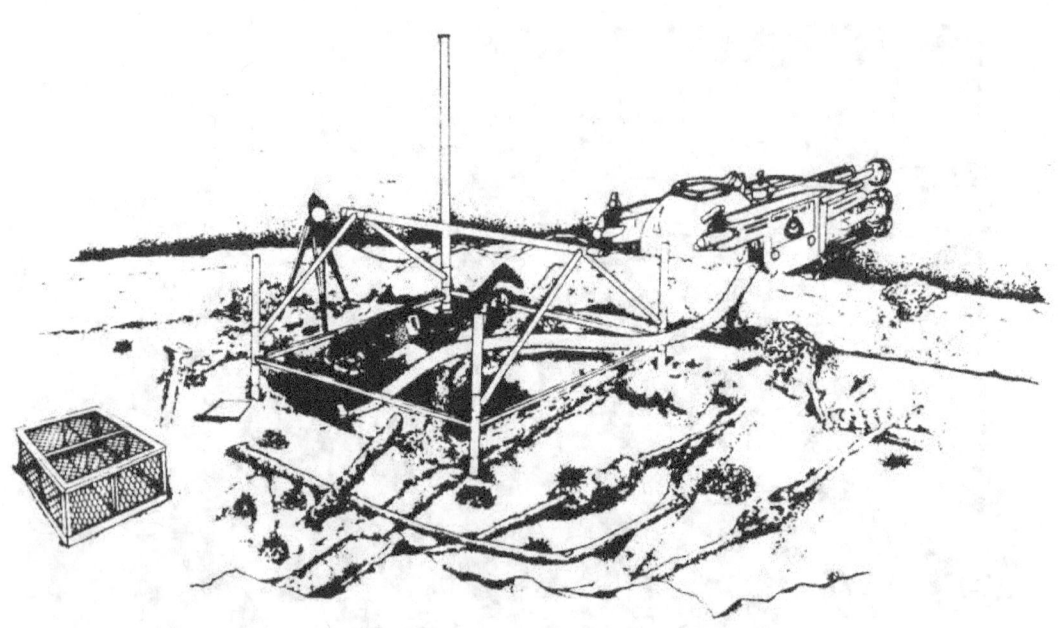

Diver investigating the interior of the MONITOR.

Systematic archaeological investigation of the wreckage can provide an opportunity to examine aspects of our past that are not recorded in surviving manuscript sources. Study of the warship can supply valuable information about the design and construction of the vessel that has come to represent the historic mid-nineteenth century transition in naval architecture and warfare. Analysis of material from the MONITOR affords rare insight into the technological development of an industrial society. Artifacts from the ship's stores and personal property of the crew can greatly enhance our understanding of life aboard the United States Navy's first ironclad warship.

MONITOR 115

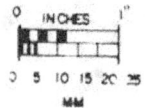

Over 108 artifacts were recovered from the excavation conducted in 1979, including a white ceramic soap dish (above) and a Hartwell's glass storage jar with lid and rubber seal (below).

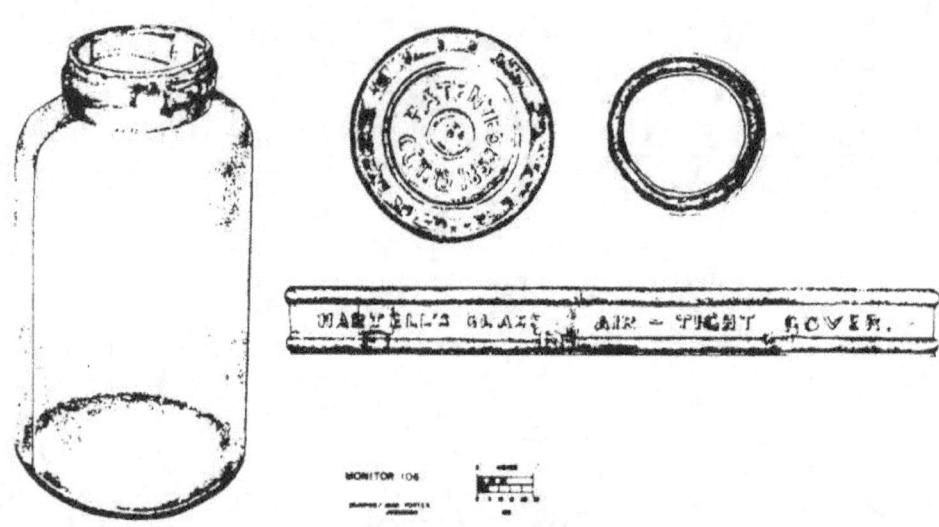

MONITOR 106

In this management plan, NOAA has set forth a policy for the management of the MONITOR National Marine Sanctuary that recognizes the importance of the MONITOR as an irreplaceable cultural resource. This management plan represents an effort to provide an integrated program of preservation, research and interpretation for an underwater archaeological site. As such, it is imperative that management-related research activities be designed in accordance with the systematic methodology of the archaeological discipline. An archaeological approach is essential for ensuring the greatest return of information, and the preservation of the wreck and its associated artifacts in a manner that will enhance its national significance. Archaeological research will enable NOAA, the on-site manager, and interested professionals to better evaluate the options for long-term management of the sanctuary.

This management plan introduces research objectives so that parties interested in the MONITOR may plan effectively and contribute both to determining the proper disposition of the wreck and to the basic store of knowledge regarding this unique resource.

To date, the following management options for the MONITOR National Marine Sanctuary have been identified. These options do not necessarily reflect final management decisions. The implementation of any one option will not preclude reevaluation of other options in light of new technological application in conservation, engineering, marine salvage, or environmental determination.

One option is that of noninterference with the wreck site. This would preclude destructive on-site research activities.

Another option is to continue limited on-site investigation and provide controlled public access to the site in a manner that will not compromise the archaeological integrity and historical value of the shipwreck. Through the review system, proposals would be approved to collect data and small artifacts that answer specific historical, archaeological, engineering and conservation questions.

Another option is to conduct partial or selective recovery of the remains of the MONITOR. Through the review system proposals would be approved for systematic recovery, conservation, interpretation and display of the remains of the MONITOR and all associated artifacts.

Another option, complete recovery of the wreck for preservation, interpretation, and display, shall be held open as a management decision until such time that all data that can be reasonably gathered on the wreck and its environment has been accumulated and analyzed.

Because of the complex nature of addressing these options, decisions will be made by NOAA based on the recommendations from the Federal Review Committee, the North Carolina Division of Archives and History and its Technical Advisory Committee and any qualified scientific parties with an interest in the management of the MONITOR National Marine Sanctuary (see Appendix D). The interdisciplinary task force will review site-related data and recommend the most viable option(s) in terms of long-range preservation, data return, determination of environmental conditions, funding, existing technology, acceptable methodology in archaeology, engineering and conservation, museology, interpretation, and economics.

On November 9, 1982, the Technical Advisory Committee resolved and recommended to NOAA that the option to recover the vessel be adopted as a major goal in the sanctuary management plan. That resolution was stated as follows:

> In keeping with the primary goals of protection and preservation of the MONITOR and all its associated records, documents and archaeological collections and to insure that the public of this and future generations have maximum access to the U.S.S. MONITOR, including its artifacts and other data, the MONITOR Technical Advisory Committee of the MONITOR National Marine Sanctuary resolves and recommends to NOAA that a major goal in the management plan for the sanctuary be the recovery of the vessel from the wreck site and its removal to an appropriate location for study, conservation and display.

The Technical Advisory Committee will be responsible for adopting and formulating plans that will detail every stage in the development of this management option. Proposals for research in the sanctuary will be submitted through the existing review process for evaluation and then sent to NOAA for approval. NOAA will evaluate the proposals in light of the potential for future research and their ability to strengthen the preservation and interpretive goals that have been outlined in this document.

This MONITOR Sanctuary Management Plan describes the sanctuary's goals and objectives and the activities to be undertaken to meet these goals.

MANAGEMENT SCHEMATIC

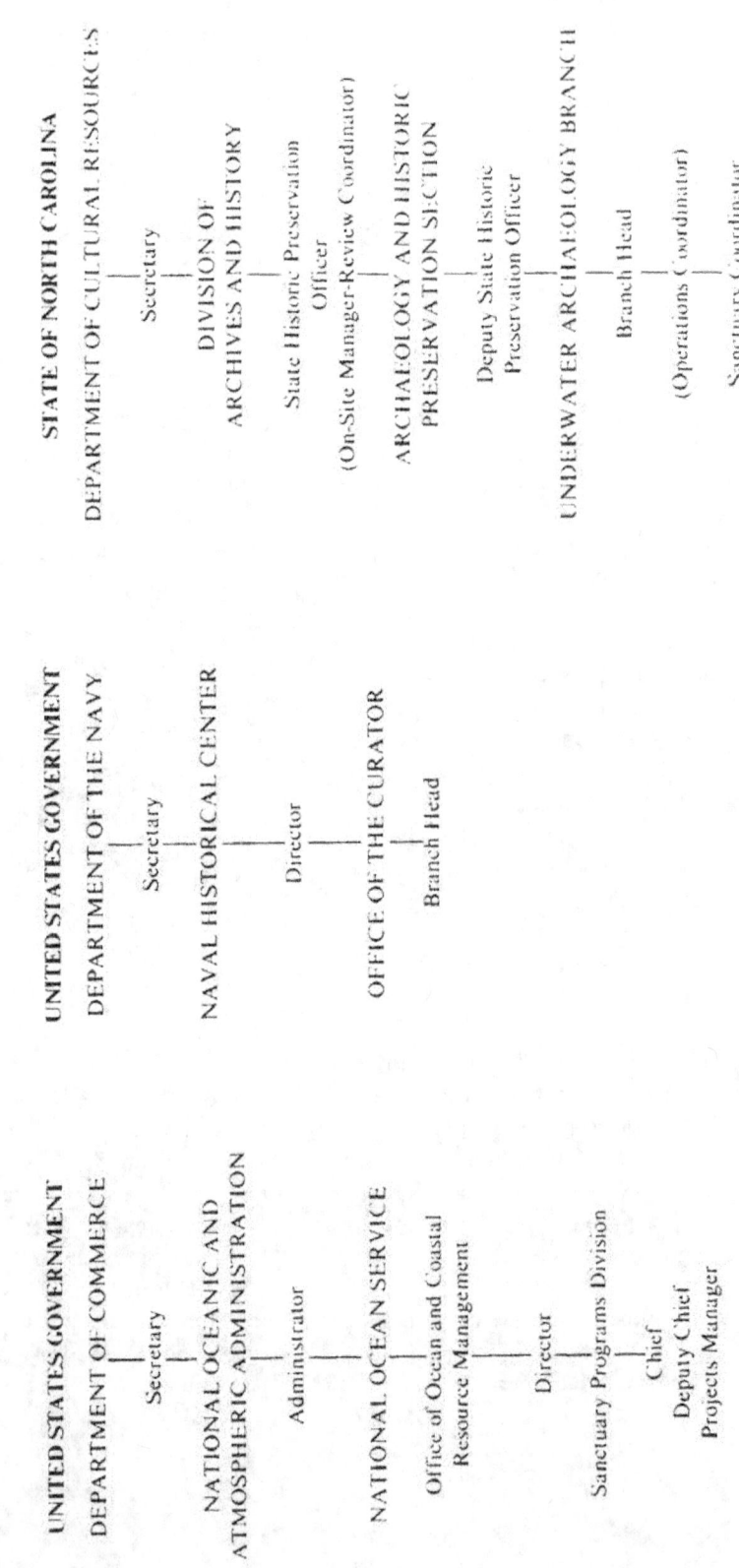

UNITED STATES GOVERNMENT
DEPARTMENT OF COMMERCE
Secretary

NATIONAL OCEANIC AND ATMOSPHERIC ADMINISTRATION
Administrator

NATIONAL OCEAN SERVICE
Office of Ocean and Coastal Resource Management
Director

Sanctuary Programs Division
Chief
Deputy Chief
Projects Manager

UNITED STATES GOVERNMENT
DEPARTMENT OF THE NAVY
Secretary

NAVAL HISTORICAL CENTER
Director

OFFICE OF THE CURATOR
Branch Head

STATE OF NORTH CAROLINA
DEPARTMENT OF CULTURAL RESOURCES
Secretary

DIVISION OF ARCHIVES AND HISTORY
State Historic Preservation Officer
(On-Site Manager-Review Coordinator)

ARCHAEOLOGY AND HISTORIC PRESERVATION SECTION
Deputy State Historic Preservation Officer

UNDERWATER ARCHAEOLOGY BRANCH
Branch Head
(Operations Coordinator)
Sanctuary Coordinator

MONITOR Technical Advisory Committee Members

11

MONITOR Federal Review Committee Members

Mr. Calvin R. Cummings
Chief
Branch of Cultural Resources
Denver Service Center, TMW
National Park Service
P.O. Box 25287
Denver, CO 80225
303 234-6112

Dr. Phillip K. Lundeberg, Curator
Division of Naval History
National Museum of American History
Washington, DC 20560
202 357-2249

Mr. Charles McKinney
National Park Service
U.S. Department of the Interior
Washington, DC 20240
202/272-3754

Dr. Forrest C. Poque, Director
Dwight D. Eisenhower Institute
  for Historical Research
Room 4027, NMAH
Smithsonian Institution
Washington, DC 20560
202 357-2183

Mr. Henry A. Vadnais, Jr.
Branch Head
Office of the Curator
Naval Historical Center
Washington Navy Yard
Washington, DC 20374
202 433-2318

Captain Harry Allendorfer
Director, Maritime Preservation
National Trust for Historic Preservation
1785 Massachusetts Avenue, N.W.
Washington, DC 20036
202 673-4127

Rear Admiral John D. Costello
Commander, 5th Coast Guard District
Federal Building
431 Crawford Street
Portsmouth, VA 23705
804/398-6000

Commander T. A. Damon
Naval Memorial Museum
Washington Navy Yard
Building 76
Washington, DC 20374
202/433-3519

Mr. Robert R. Garvey, Jr.
Executive Director
Advisory Council on Historic Preservation
1522 K Street, N.W.
Washington, DC 20005
202/254-3974

Admiral John D. H. Kane, Jr.
Curator for the Navy
Naval Historical Center
Washington Navy Yard
Building 57
Washington, DC 20374
202/433-2210

U.S.S. MONITOR NATIONAL MARINE SANCTUARY MANAGEMENT PLAN

INTRODUCTION

Title III of the Marine Protection, Research and Sanctuaries Act of 1972 (16 U.S.C. 1431-1434, Section 302a) authorizes the Secretary of Commerce, after consultation with appropriate Federal agencies and the affected state, and following Presidential approval, to designate ocean waters as marine sanctuaries for the purpose of preserving their distinctive conservation, recreational, ecological, cultural, and esthetic values. The Act is administered by the National Oceanic and Atmospheric Administration (NOAA) through the Office of Ocean and Coastal Resource Management's National Marine Sanctuary Program.

National Marine Sanctuary Program Goals

The mission of the National Marine Sanctuary Program is to establish a system of national marine sanctuaries based on the identification, designation, and comprehensive management of special marine areas for the long-term benefit and enjoyment of the public. The overall goals of the National Sanctuary Program are:

1. Enhance resource protection through the implementation of a comprehensive, long-term management plan tailored to the specific resources.

2. Promote and coordinate research to expand scientific knowledge of significant marine resources and improve management decision-making.

3. Enhance public awareness, understanding, and wise use of the marine environment through public interpretive and recreational programs.

4. Provide for maximum compatible public and private use of special marine areas.

Site Designation Background

In September 1974, the State of North Carolina nominated the site of the MONITOR, which lies in 220 feet of water 16 miles off Cape Hatteras, North Carolina, for marine sanctuary status to protect the wreck from unauthorized activities. The official designation of the Nation's first national marine sanctuary was made by NOAA on January 30, 1975.

Designation of the MONITOR site as a national marine sanctuary recognizes its importance as an irreplaceable cultural resource. A properly managed sanctuary will protect and preserve the MONITOR as a unique part of the national heritage in a way that will enable the MONITOR to be both meaningful and accessible to the public, as well as scientific researchers. Therefore, NOAA's coordination with citizens, scientific organizations, and North Carolina and Federal agencies is important in developing a sanctuary management plan that expresses goals, objectives, and tasks that will enhance the MONITOR's value as a source of historic and scientific information. This management plan for the MONITOR National Marine Sanctuary will be reviewed and updated annually.

SANCTUARY RESOURCES AND USES

Environmental Setting

The remains of the MONITOR lie on the Continental Shelf 16.1 miles south-southeast of the Cape Hatteras Light. The MONITOR National Marine Sanctuary consists of a vertical column of water in the Atlantic Ocean one nautical mile in diameter extending from the surface to the seabed. The center of the water column is 35° 00' 23" north latitude and 75° 24' 32" west longitude. In the vicinity of the wreckage the ocean bottom is composed of sand, shell hash and clay below the surface. Bathymetric profiles of the area indicate that the bottom surface slopes gently away to the southeast.

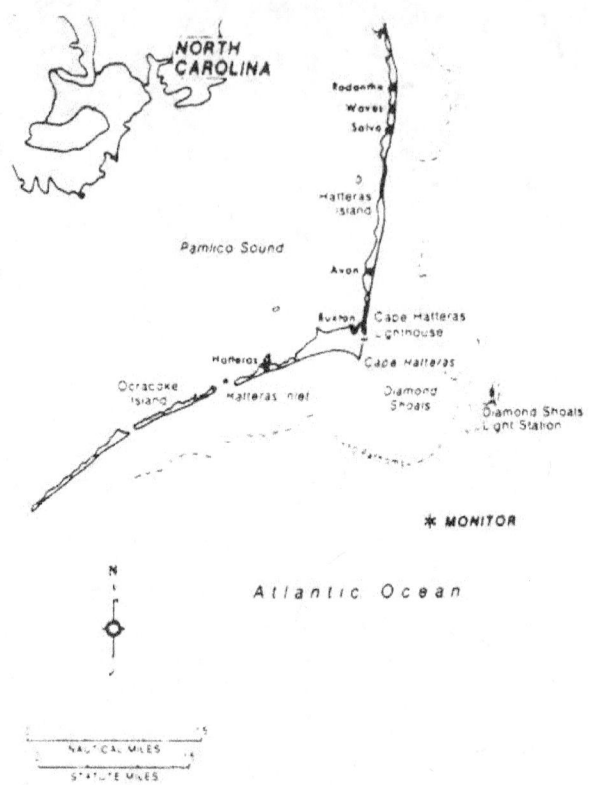

(Drawing by Sherry King)

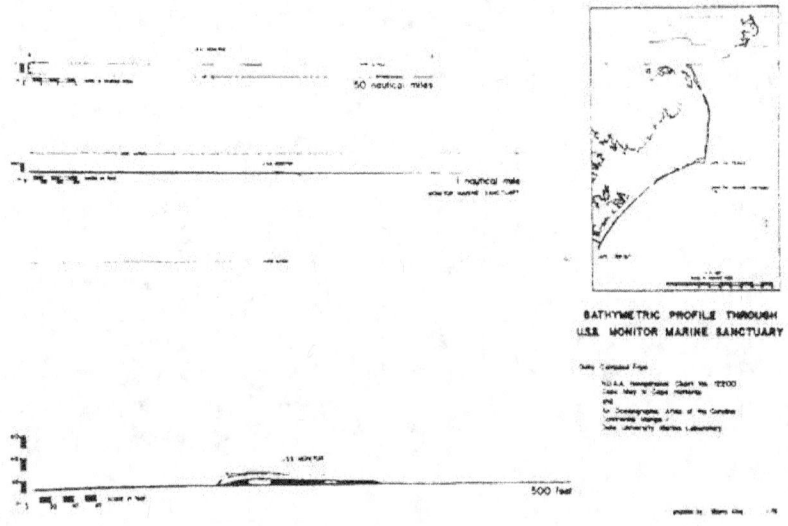

A bathymetric profile illustrates the wreck's relationship to the Continental Shelf and the gentle slope of the sea floor through the sanctuary.
(Drawing by Sherry King)

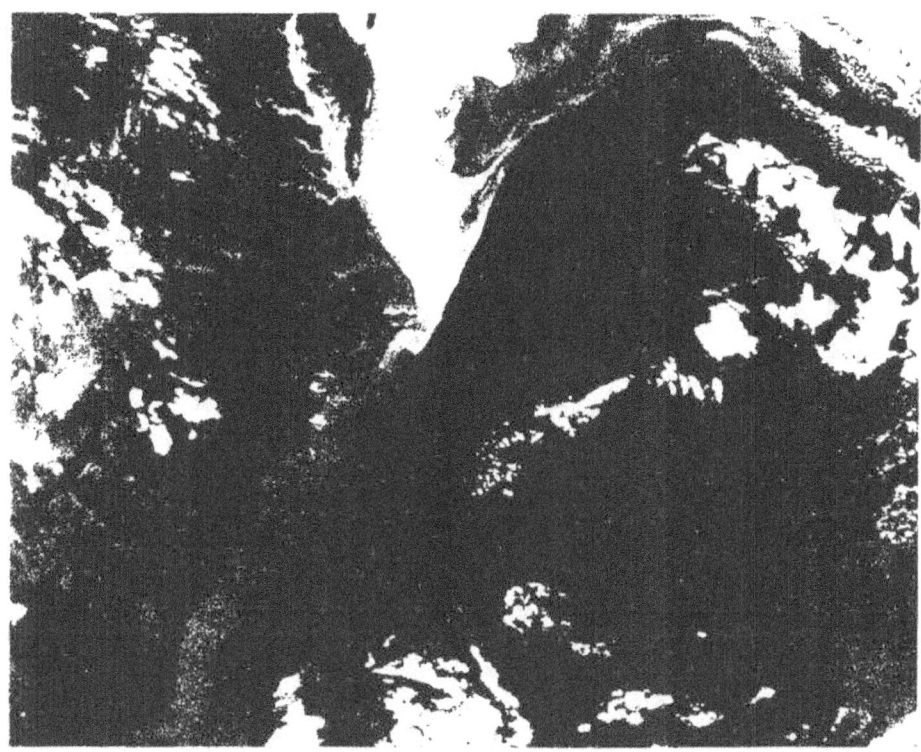

While the MONITOR is thought to be outside the western margin of the Gulf Stream, counter currents and eddies influence environmental conditions at the wreck site.

Visibility in the 220 foot deep water varies according to turbidity, the presence of microorganisms, and the intensity and angle of sunlight. Records to date indicate that visibility varies from approximately 10 feet to more than 100 feet.

Although the site appears to be outside the western margin of the Gulf Stream, eddies created by that current may directly influence the area. Changes in current direction and velocity occur almost constantly. Within a 24-hour period, direction has been observed to change 360 degrees. Current velocities are known to vary from 0.02 to more than 1.5 knots at the bottom and surface currents appear to be considerably stronger. Both temperature and salinity in the area seem to be related to these current patterns. While little specific data is available, temperature projections indicate an annual variation between 11 and 20 degrees Celsius.

Wind patterns in the area of the MONITOR National Marine Sanctuary can be generalized as prevailing from the north to west between November and February; north-northwest and south-southeast between March and June; south-southeast during July and August; and north-northeast during September and October. However, unpredictable variation has been observed and spontaneous storms frequently occur.

Description of Wreck

The present condition of the MONITOR can be directly related to both damage that occurred at the time of sinking and deterioration which has resulted from more than a century of immersion in a sea water environment. The inverted hull of the warship rests partially submerged in bottom sediment with the port quarter supported by the displaced 21-1/2-foot outside diameter, 9-foot high and 8-inch thick turret.

15

Photomosaic of the wreck site made from photographs taken in 1974 by Alcoa Marine Corp.
Photomosaic courtesy of Naval Intelligence Support Center. Sketch by Steve Daniel.

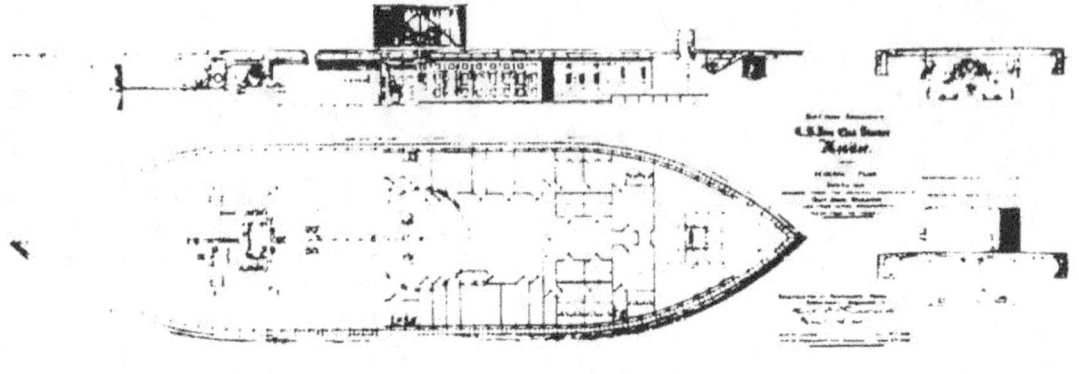

One of several frequently contradictory plans of Ericsson's MONITOR.

THE HULL

Analysis of the wreckage confirms that the condition of the aft portion of the hull differs dramatically from the remains forward of the midships bulkhead. Aft of the bulkhead, the bottom plating   ves intact. However, along both of the sloping side of the displacement hull, the plating has deteriorated and to a large degree only the remains of the iron frame survive. Above the aft overhang the distinctive skeg and propeller shaft can be traced to the propeller and support yoke. The starboard quarter is buried to a depth of approximately 5 feet while the port quarter is supported more than 7 feet above the bottom by the turret. Inside the hull, steam propulsion and auxiliary machinery has survived intact and in a good state of preservation.

16

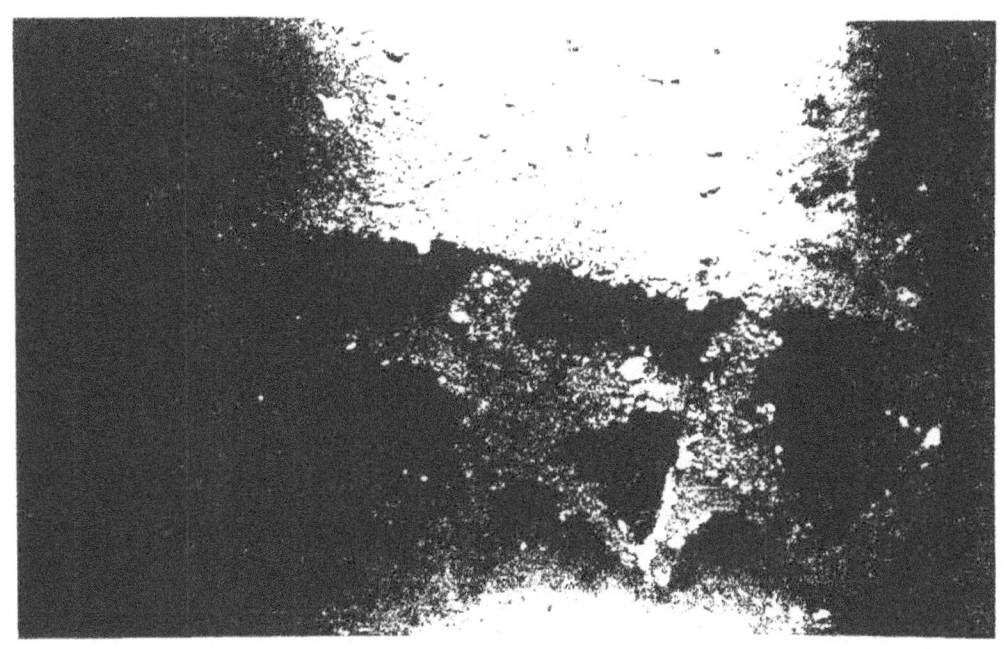

Natural deterioration of the plating exposing the framing of the starboard side of the lower hull.

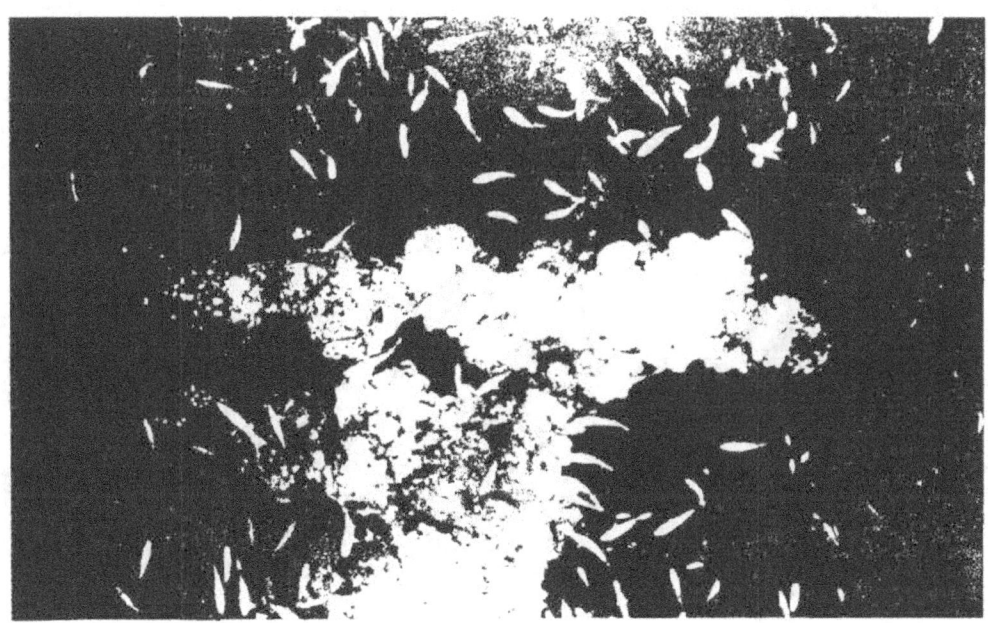

Heavy marine fouling virtually obscures the propeller located immediately below the skeg which is the highest point on the site.

*The turret, displaced during sinking, supports the port quarter of the inverted hull.
Drawing by Joan Jannama*

*A spoked wheel on one of two blower engines that were used to create a forced draft for
the boilers can be seen from the port side.
·Photography by Gordon Watts·*

Forward of the midships bulkhead, damage to the lower hull is extensive. Although displaced sections of lower hull plating exist along the starboard side, no intact plating has been identified along the port side. In fact, much of the material in evidence along the port side has been identified as portions of the interior of the ship or equipment and fittings that were stowed below the crew's quarters, ward room, and galley. From the circular anchor well immediately aft of the bow, anchor chain leads over the hull and into the bottom sediment to the south. Aft of the anchor well, the deck beams that support the pilot house are visible. Although most of the armor belt on the starboard side is buried, its stable condition is evident at the bow and along the port side.

Although incomplete, the data available indicated that the destruction of the lower hull forward of the midships bulkhead closely resembles that which results from an explosion of considerable force. As the site is located in the traditional shipping lane off the North Carolina coast, it is possible that the damage is the result of the effects of depth charge attacks during

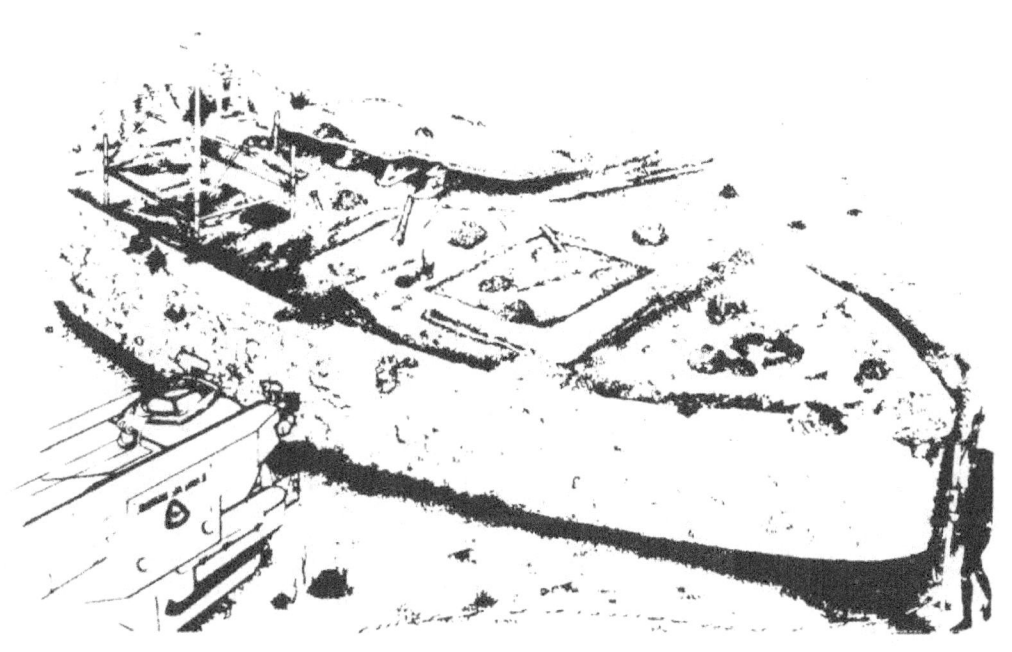

Damage to the lower hull forward of the midships bulkhead is extensive.
(Drawing by Joan Jannaman)

Artist's rendering of the remains of the U.S.S. MONITOR.

19

World War II. During the war enemy submarines frequently rested on the shallow bottom of the continental shelf during the day, surfacing at night to destroy merchant shipping along the coast. In an effort to prevent this, the Navy and Coast Guard made a practice of dropping depth charges on all sonar targets. Quite possibly one of these targets could have been the MONITOR. An explosion of this type in the area forward of the midships bulkhead would certainly have been capable of collapsing the already weakened hull of the vessel, and may also explain the distribution of hull plates yards from the wreck.

THE DECK

Forward of the pilot house, virtually all of the deck is free of the bottom sediment. The lower 12 inches of the pilot house structure is exposed above the sediment. From this point aft to the present position of the turret, the entire port side of the vessel remains free of the bottom, supporting its own weight and that of the sediment accumulated within the confines of the hull. Aft of the engineering space, the deck has suffered extensive damage and considerably less of the deck there supports itself. The armor plating on the deck is separated from the deck planking in several areas, indicating advanced deterioration.

At both the wardroom and midships locations where the deck of the MONITOR is ruptured, material associated with the ship is washing out of the wreck and onto the sediment below. The amount of material redistributed in this manner appeared to be augmented by pressure created by the current flowing over the wreck.

In the vicinity of the turret, deck plates have been dislodged by destruction associated with the stern of the vessel. Behind the turret the deck has, in fact, completely separated and armor plates hang suspended by deteriorated fittings. Forward of the turret, deck armor plates are generally in their original position and distrubance is slight. Below the position of the port boiler uptake hatch, a portion of the smokepipe breaching is protruding from the deck and into the sediment.

THE TURRET

Structurally the remains of the turret are in excellent condition. The gun ports are blocked by heavy wrought iron port stoppers that protected the ordnance and gun crew from hostile fire. Wood bucklers that covered the gun ports while underway are not present, although bolts that held them in place are intact and protrude from the rammer holes in the port stoppers. Aside from basketball-size dents still visible through the heavy fouling, little damage is apparent. Probing the turret floor with a 3-foot compressed gas probe during the 1979 expedition indicated that the wood floor of the structure has deteriorated but remains intact under a layer of sediment and coral. Examination of the structure produced no indication of access hatches in the base. A depression in the center of the turret floor indicated that the shaft upon which the turret rotated had dislodged as the turret and hull separated.

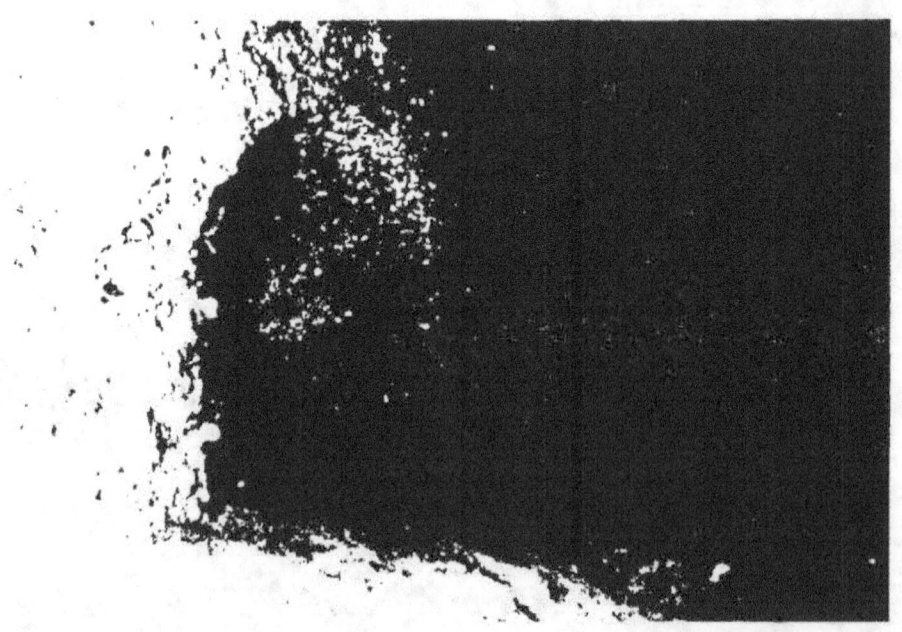

Gun ports, blocked by iron port stoppers, are visible above the sand bottom.
(Photograph by Gordon Watts)

Gordon P. Watts, Jr., underwater archaeologist, works with photographic equipment used to record the 1979 archaeological expedition to the MONITOR sanctuary.

For a more detailed description of the MONITOR site, please refer to "Investigating the Remains of the U.S.S. MONITOR: A Final Report on 1979 Site Testing in the MONITOR Marine Sanctuary". The 1979 expedition was jointly sponsored by NOAA, the State of North Carolina, and Harbor Branch Foundation of Fort Pierce, Florida. The report was prepared by North Carolina's Underwater Archaeology Branch and is available upon request from NOAA's Sanctuary Programs Division in Washington, D.C.

THE PLAN

Sanctuary Management Plans include six elements:

A. Goals and Objectives—Site-specific goals and objectives tailored to the sanctuary.

B. Administration—An administrative section that describes the sanctuary's daily operations and the responsibilities of NOAA and the site manager.

C. Resource Studies—A comprehensive resource studies plan that identifies data gaps, focuses on management related research, and assigns priorities.

D. Interpretation—An interpretive plan designed to communicate the significance of the resources being protected.

E. Surveillance and Enforcement.

F. Regulations.

Goals and Objectives

Site-specific goals provide the framework within which sanctuary management activities are structured. These goals are normally long-term and somewhat open-ended with specific objectives tailored to short-term sanctuary needs and formulated in accordance with the National Marine Sanctuary Program's overall goals.

The U.S.S. MONITOR National Marine Sanctuary goals and objectives are:

Goal 1—To protect and preserve the MONITOR and all of its associated records, documents and archaeological collections.

Objective—Design and implement a management plan with an effective administrative system to insure long-term protection of the site.

Goal 2—To insure the systematic scientific recovery and dissemination of historical and cultural information preserved at the MONITOR site; and to preserve and develop the physical remains of the

21

Vessels used during the 1979 expedition were the R/V JOHNSON (above) and the submersible JOHNSON SEA LINK (below), supplied by Harbor Branch Foundation of Fort Pierce, Florida.

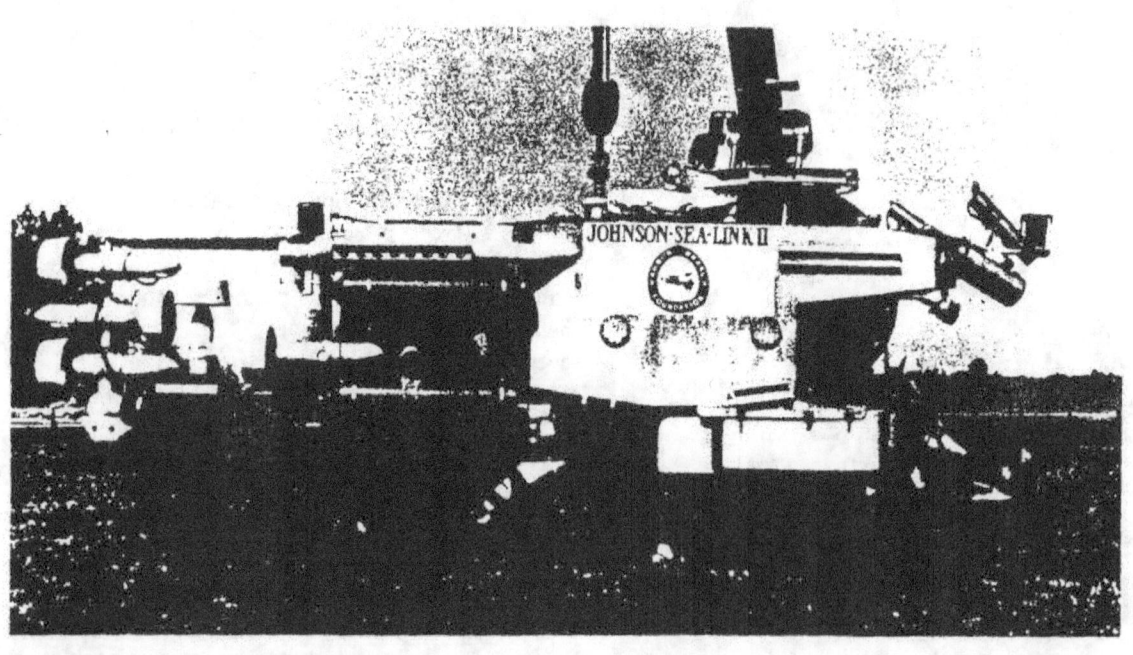

MONITOR in a manner which appropriately enhances both the significance and interpretive potential of the warship remains.

Objective—Develop a resource studies plan for the MONITOR which establishes methods for:
1) Assimilating data
2) Defining research alternatives.
3) Identifying future alternative management options for the site.

Goal 3—To enhance public awareness and understanding of the MONITOR as a historic and cultural resource by providing interpretive educational services and materials.

Objective—
1) Develop appropriate publications.
2) Provide written, audiovisual, and other materials as appropriate to communicate the historical and cultural message of the MONITOR.
3) Explore new communication approaches to bringing the MONITOR closer to the general public.

In reality, these three site-specific goals greatly overlap each other. Effective preservation can only be carried out through comprehensive administration of the MONITOR site (see Protection and Preservation Section) and through proper conservation and curation of artifacts removed from the wreck. Care for MONITOR artifacts will be provided by NOAA, the North Carolina Division of Archives and History (DAH) and the Curator for the U.S. Navy (Appendix C: Policy for Management of MONITOR Collections).

Administration

NOAA and the State of North Carolina (N.C.) cooperatively manage the site of the U.S.S. MONITOR through an agreement which designates the N.C. Department of Cultural Resources, Division of Archives and History as on-site manager.

Under this Cooperative Agreement the State provides the following:

- A sanctuary coordinator position at the N.C. Underwater Archaeology Branch, Kure Beach, N.C.;
- On-site implementation of the management plan;
- An annual review, with the MONITOR Federal Review Committee and the State of North Carolina Technical Advisory Committee (TAC) of current research proposals and recommendations for refinement of the proposal review system;
- A review of and recommendations to NOAA for action on permit applications;
- A record of sanctuary research and status of ongoing projects;

- Coordination with the U.S. Coast Guard regarding surveillance and enforcement;
- Submission of periodic administrative reports to NOAA;
- Annual review of the MONITOR Sanctuary Management Plan with NOAA;
- Assistance in selection of qualified technical reviewers for research proposals and maintains communication among reviewers.

NOAA's Sanctuary Programs Division (SPD) is responsible for management of all of the National Marine Sanctuaries. SPD responsibilities for the MONITOR National Marine Sanctuary include:

- Development of sanctuary goals and objectives and the overall management plan;
- Supervision of on-site implementation of the management plan;
- Issuance of all sanctuary permits;
- Funding of management plan implementation;
- Development and implementation of a policy for administering and managing the collection of artifacts from the MONITOR Sanctuary (Appendix C: Policy for Management of MONITOR Collections);
- Annual review and revision of the sanctuary management plan to include new research data that affect management decisions.

In addition, NOAA and the Department of the Navy signed a Memorandum of Understanding (MOU) to the effect that the Curator for the Navy will provide curatorial services for the artifacts recovered from the MONITOR National Marine Sanctuary.

Under this MOU the Curator for the U.S. Navy:

- Provides curatorial services required for the proper management and control of the artifacts recovered from the MONITOR Sanctuary (Appendix C: Policy for Management of MONITOR Collections).
- Develops and maintains a continuous register of the MONITOR collections.
- Manages loans, exhibitions and storage of the MONITOR artifacts.
- Assists NOAA in the review of applications requesting loan of MONITOR artifacts.

As a vital part of all management activities, interagency cooperation will play a major role in this plan. NOAA will insure coordination and cooperation among all agencies involved in MONITOR sanctuary management activities, especially administration and enforcement.

NOAA will maintain an ad hoc Federal Committee consisting of representatives from the U.S. Coast Guard; Department of the Interior; U.S. Navy; the Smithsonian Institution; National Trust for Historical Preservation;

and the Advisory Council for Historic Preservation for advice and technical assistance concerning:

- Design and implementation of MONITOR research projects;
- Review of research permits; and,
- Setting priorities for management goals, objectives and tasks.

Resources Studies Plan

The wreckage and associated artifacts that the remains of the MONITOR preserve represent historical and cultural data as well as a rare collection of physical evidence from a dramatic period in American history. The psychological impact of the MONITOR's successful engagement with the VIRGINIA swept the warship from relative obscurity to a position of international attention. The MONITOR's celebrated "victory" at Hampton Roads assured the naval vessel a reputation achieved by no other ship of the United States Navy. The past century has by no means diluted this interest and attention. Properly investigated, preserved, and displayed, the MONITOR can become an unparalleled national resource offering scientific, historical, educational and recreational opportunities for American people. NOAA, together with the North Carolina sanctuary on-site manager, contributes toward public understanding of the contemporary research conducted at the sanctuary through publication and dissemination of research findings.

NOAA generally will not provide financial support for research expeditions in the MONITOR Sanctuary. However, availability of funds permitting, NOAA will consider proposals for limited assistance towards some research-related activities, such as financing analysis of data or cost of publications.

Research is essential to the acquisition of data that contribute directly to resolving management, interpretation, protection, and preservation problems in the MONITOR Sanctuary. Therefore, the research goal of this management plan outlines research objectives and tasks that serve as a guide to the systematic development of research projects that yield data of the highest priority. Persons interested in developing alternative proposals can receive technical assistance from NOAA and the North Carolina site manager. At the present time NOAA will encourage and give highest priority to research proposals that contribute to responsible option assessment and yield the following types of information:

- Historical data through archival records and on-site investigation to enable development of comprehensive depiction of the MONITOR as the vessel existed on December 31, 1862.

- Archaeological data that contributes towards the development of an adequate model of the nature and disposition of the wreck and its associated artifacts through application of systematic principles of underwater archaeology.
- Environmental-oceanographic data that contributes towards a better understanding of the effects the environment has on the preservation of the wreck *in situ* and on any on-site activities.
- Engineering studies to determine missing design and construction information for the vessel, methods for deployment of equipment and personnel on deepwater archaeological sites, and development of predictive models on the effects of alternative recovery methods for the wreck or its selected features.
- Conservation data to identify preservation problems with the wreck *in situ* and development of predictive models on the problems encountered with recovery, stabilization and display of the wreck and its associated artifacts.
- Public benefit through research and educational activities including publications, films, photographs, public lectures and museum exhibits. Public educational efforts should provide the means to communicate the sanctuary's rules and regulations; present to the public the history and nature of scientific research activities on the MONITOR; and make available research data on the MONITOR to the scientific community at large.

All future activities in the MONITOR Sanctuary involving potential recovery of material from the site will include provisions for cleaning, conservation, and storage of the material, including adequate staff, facilities, equipment, supplies, and budget. In addition, due to the historical importance of the vessel and its value as a unique cultural resource, every effort will be made to provide public access to any recovered material in the form of exhibits.

Management of the MONITOR Sanctuary involves a continuous process of refining management decisions as research provides new baseline data that contribute toward accomplishing the sanctuary objectives. Consequently, a primary consideration of all agencies and parties interested in the MONITOR should be to investigate and understand the environment, condition and structure of the wreck and make their analyses available to the public and scientific community.

This MONITOR sanctuary management plan serves to assist experts in their respective fields in planning research, and once accumulation and analysis of sufficient information on the MONITOR has been accomplished, NOAA will be able to evaluate more fully future research and/or recovery options. From this process a decision relating to the MONITOR's proper disposition will emerge that assures preservation of the values protected by the sanctuary.

The current Resources Studies Plan lists those priority projects underway or planned for FY 83; and identifies those already suggested for the future, provided that funds are available and adequate interest is demonstrated by the public and the research community. Many of these studies are interrelated and could be conducted simultaneously. The current Resources Studies list does not preclude the introduction of additional studies.

List of Resources Studies

1. Analysis of water conditions and sea state.
2. Study of currents, visibility, erosion, depositional patterns, and the nature of the water column in the MONITOR Sanctuary.
3. Surface and sub-surface sediment studies.
4. On-site engineering and structural data collection.
5. Establish an on-site provenience system.
6. Continued site definition.
7. On-site test excavations.
8. Location, documentation and recovery of the anchor.
9. Investigation of the interior of the turret.
10. Develop a conservation plan, including procedures, and facilities necessary for conservation, curation and display of material recovered from the wreck.
11. Conduct a photogrammetric analysis of existing stereo photography.
12. Produce a photographic index of 1977 NOAA—HARBOR BRANCH FOUNDATION explorations of the MONITOR site.
13. An engineering structural assessment of the MONITOR.
14. On-site collection of ship's structure data.
15. Determination of the rate of deterioration of the remains of the MONITOR.
16. Compile a catalog of existing plans and drawings of the MONITOR. Completion of a comprehensive set of engineering drawings from the above catalog, and determination of the necessary information that exists only at the site.
17. Archival study and location of the ship's contents.

Resources Studies

1. *Study Title:* Analysis of water conditions and sea state.
   Information Needs: A survey of the existing weather and environmental records pertaining to the Hat-teras area and the development of a comprehensive model of the annual weather conditions will be an invaluable aid to on-site research.

2. *Study Title:* Study of currents, visibility, erosion, depositional patterns, and the nature of the water column in the MONITOR Sanctuary.
   Information Needs: An environmental definition of the MONITOR site is necessary for two reasons. First, to determine the effect of the environment on the wreck, and second, to assist in the planning and conduct of on-site research. The deployment and maintenance of current meter arrays, the collection of water column analysis data (e.g., Salinity, Temperature, Depth [STD], oxygen content, suspended particulate matter) and the collation of these data will assist in determining the conditions encountered during on-site archaeological research.

3. *Study Title:* Surface and sub-surface sediment studies.
   Information Needs: Analysis of the character of the sediments will assist in determining methods and techniques for use in large-scale excavation at the site.

4. *Study Title:* On site collection of ship's structure data.
   Information Needs: To verify and/or establish the location and nature of internal and external features that cannot be documented through historical or archival research.

5. *Study Title:* Establish an on-site provenience system.
   Information Needs: To tie additional research to a master grid, the placement of a series of datum casings, initiated during the 1979 expedition to the site, should be completed.

6. *Study Title:* Continued site definition.
   Information Needs: To produce an acoustic, magnetic, bathymetric, seismic and videographic record of the site that will define bottom and sub-bottom conditions, and to locate and identify material associated with the wreck but existing outside the confines of the hull remains.

7. *Study Title:* On-site test excavations.
   Information Needs: To evaluate the nature and extent of the archaeological record, test excavations both inside and outside the confines of the hull could generate historical, engineering and environmental data that would expand knowledge of the wreck site and its environment.

8. *Study Title:* Location, documentation and recovery of the anchor.
   Information Needs: Recovery of the anchor will provide archaeologists with insight into the methods and techniques necessary to locate, document,

recover and conserve large objects associated with the MONITOR site, information on the condition of other similar material at the site and a study of sedimentation in the MONITOR Sanctuary since December 31, 1862.

9. *Study Title:* Investigation of the interior of the turret.
   Information Needs: To accurately establish the contents and conditions of the turret for the development and assessment of turret recovery operations.

10. *Study Title:* Develop a conservation plan, including procedures, and facilities necessary for conservation, curation and display of material recovered from the wreck, for each of the following options.
    a) Continued limited collection of small artifacts.
    b) Partial or selected recovery of portion of the wreck.
    c) Complete recovery of the wreck.
    Information Needs: To insure that all material recovered from the site will undergo proper conservation and to provide a facility for continued conservation and display of the artifacts.

11. *Study Title:* Conduct a photogrammetric analysis of existing stereo photography.
    Information Needs: To generate horizontal and vertical profiles and produce a photomosaic of the wreck site.

12. *Study Title:* Produce a photographic index of 1977 NOAA-HARBOR BRANCH FOUNDATION explorations of the MONITOR site. (Completed: 1981.)
    Information Needs: To provide researchers with a catalog of existing photographs that can be used for historical research, and the planning and operation of future research at the site. (Contracted to: Edward M. Miller, Annapolis, Maryland.)

13. *Study Title:* An engineering structural assessment of the MONITOR (Completed: December, 1981.)
    Information Needs: Before plans for the recovery of the MONITOR can be considered, it will be necessary to identify and define specific on-site engineering data that must be collected and analyzed to determine feasible, suitable and acceptable recovery options. These data will be utilized to determine the techniques for the recovery of the MONITOR or portions of the vessel structure. Engineering studies and on-site data collection will be designed to assess the nature and extent of structural damage to the hull. (Contracted to: Dr. Bruce Muga, Durham, North Carolina.)

14. *Study Title:* On-site engineering and structural data collection.
    Information Needs: To perform the necessary *in situ* measurements to answer the questions generated by the above engineering assessment, specifically:

* Examine the condition of the turret
  a. Determine the degree of corrosive welding between the turret bearing surface and the armor belt and estimate the actual contact area.
  b. Note any nicks, bends, striations or chatter marks on the turret and armor belt that could constitute evidence of long-term settlement or differential movement of the turret and hull.
  c. Determine the turret's deviation from vertical with a pitch and/or roll gauge, taking several measurements around the periphery of the turret.
  d. Measure the clearance between the turret and the port armor belt on the downstream side.
  e. Note any appendages that might restrict free movement of the turret. If any appendages are present, the nature of the connections and the effort necessary to disengage them should be determined.
  f. Determine the condition of the interior of the turret, its contents and the degree of siltation.
  g. Examine the condition of the turret roof to determine if the roof and roof beams can tolerate the abrasive forces during sliding/dragging operations. This can be accomplished by visual inspection from the turret interior or by excavation adjacent to the turret on the downstream side.
  h. Determine the nature and condition of the soil in the vicinity of and exterior to the turret along the movement path. A minimum of 4 borings to a depth of at least 6 inches below the turret roof should be taken and the presence or absence of any obstruction should be noted.

2) Determine the competency of the 10" by 10" oak deck beam main frame members.
  a. Determine the degree of deterioration of the beams by visual inspection in conjunction with physical probing, noting local discolorations, surface perforations and average penetration distances to competent material.
  b. Remove a 4-foot or longer section of one of the already damaged beams that can be used to conduct strength tests under controlled laboratory conditions. These tests should include axial stress, shear stress and bending stress tests, and transverse and longitudinal wave propagation tests.

c. Conduct either a one decay tests on two beams at least 18-feet long or place one or more of the deck beams in axial compression and measure the differential movements at selected locations. These tests will determine any undetected beam damage resulting from large-scale causes such as initial capsizing, depth charge or physical decay of the material.

3) Evaluate the adequacy of the connections.
   a. Examine the area around the bolts, pins or spikes which join the oak deck beams to the port armor belt bracket for evidence of splitting of the beam or deterioration of the beam or connector.
   b. Examine the spike connections which join the deck plates to the oak deck beams. Spike head diameters should be measured and the degree of corrosive welding should be noted.
   c. Conduct pushing or pulling tests either in the field or laboratory to determine the maximum load necessary to initiate movement.
   d. Conduct pulling tests of a specially designed high capacity magnet to determine the possibility of enhancing the strength of existing members and the critical connections.

15. *Study Title:* Determination of the rate of deterioration of the remains of the MONITOR (Completed: January, 1983).
    Information Needs: To determine the current rate of natural deterioration of the wreck to assist in the evaluation of management options. (Contracted to: Edward M. Miller, Annapolis, Maryland.)

16. *Study Title:* Compile a catalog of existing plans and drawings of the MONITOR (Completed: 1982).
    Information Needs: Completion of a comprehensive set of engineering drawings from the above catalog, and determination of the necessary information that exists only at the site. (Contracted to: Ernest W. Peterkin, Camp Springs, Maryland.)

Today the remains of John Ericsson's "Cheesebox-on-a-Raft" represents a unique legacy from the past. The shipwreck and its contents preserve an irreplaceable historical record and represent a monument to the American naval tradition the MONITOR helped to create. There is no accurate set of plans of the MONITOR as it existed on December 31, 1862. Through studies of contemporary drawings and on-site research it will

be possible to develop a comprehensive demo of the MONITOR. The drawings that are produced by these studies will be invaluable for future historical, archaeological and engineering assessments of the wreck.

17. *Study Title:* Archival study and location of the ship's contents (Completed: 1983).
    Information Needs: To accurately assess the archaeological record preserved at the site it will be necessary to determine the nature, extent and location of the ship's stores fittings, equipment, ordnance and personal effects aboard the MONITOR at the time of its sinking. (Contracted to: Ernest W. Peterkin, Camp Springs, Maryland.)

List of Interpretive Programs

A. Publications
   1. Activities Report: "CHEESEBOX"
   2. "Information for Potential Researchers"
   3. Copies of conference papers
   4. Expedition reports, operations manuals, and analytical and technical reports

B. Materials oriented toward teaching institutions
   1. MONITOR educational material for middle or secondary school levels
   2. "Diver's Orientation and introduction of the MONITOR"
   3. History of the MONITOR

C. Multimedia material oriented toward reaching general public through film, videotapes, lectures, artifact loans (already existing)
   1. Scientific documentary film
   2. Traveling MONITOR exhibit
   3. Engineering model of wreck *in situ*
   4. Feasibility study for TV broadcast

Interpretive Programs

The interpretive programs for the U.S.S. MONITOR National Marine Sanctuary include the following elements:

A. Publications
   1. NOAA, DAH, and other interested parties will compile and distribute a MONITOR semi-annual activities report "CHEESEBOX" describing the current status of research activities in the sanctuary and selected episodes from the MONITOR's history. (Contracted to: Program in Maritime History and Underwater Research, East Carolina University, Greenville, North Carolina.)
   2. DAH and NOAA will develop and distribute a pamphlet, on request, entitled "Information

for Potential Researchers" describing the MONITOR Sanctuary rules and regulations and research permit procedures.

3. NOAA and DAH will develop and/or make available reprints or copies from professional conference papers regarding the MONITOR and/or underwater archaeology.

4. NOAA and DAH will develop and/or make available MONITOR expedition reports, operations manuals and analytical and technical reports.

B. Material oriented toward teaching institutions

1. *Study Title:* To develop educational material on the MONITOR for use at the middle and secondary school levels.

   Information Needs: To facilitate our country's youth in developing an appreciation of the role the MONITOR played in shaping the American naval tradition we know today. The educational material will be devoted to the MONITOR and will be generally consistent with the objectives of the national curricula regarding study of the Civil War Period. The material will be readily adaptable to either the middle or secondary school levels.

2. *Study Title:* Produce a biographical sketch of the six commanding officers of the U.S.S. MONITOR.

   Information Needs: To complement technical research on the MONITOR, a 10 to 20 page biographical sketch will be produced for each of the six officers who commanded the MONITOR during her brief history. Military and personal biographical information will be obtained from the MONITOR archives at East Carolina University as well as from private collections and State repositories.

3. *Study Title:* Conduct a search of the military and other records for information concerning the men who served aboard the U.S.S. MONITOR.

   Information Needs: To provide information concerning those who served aboard the MONITOR, military and genealogical information will be collected on each of the 125 MONITOR crewmen who have been identified to date. Military records include Pension Application Files containing an official statement of veteran's naval service, as well as information of a personal nature. Bounty-Land Warrant Application Files containing service data and the veteran's age and place of residence at the time the application was made, and MONITOR Muster Rolls containing the man's name, rank, age, state of birth, previous service, payment dates and physical description. Genealogical information will be obtained through an

advertisement in the "The Genealogical Helper", the most widely circulated genealogical magazine available, listing all crew members and requesting personal information from descendants. The final result will be a copy of all records and correspondence along with a biographical summary derived from the material obtained.

4. *Study Title:* To develop a concise curriculum guide entitled "Diver's Orientation and Introduction of the MONITOR".

   Information Needs: To develop a program to introduce and instruct divers prior to their research at the MONITOR Sanctuary regarding safety procedures, the physical arrangements of the wreck, and detailed description of locations of doors, hatches, ladders, and the probable locations of the 1500 classes of MONITOR artifacts.

5. *Study Title:* To write, compile and edit a comprehensive text on the history of the MONITOR.

   Information Needs: To provide to the public an authoritative work on the MONITOR. Authorities in the naval historical field will be requested to assist NOAA in the compilation of bibliographical and textual information for the work. The book will be an anthology of the stages of the MONITOR's life, from her conception by John Ericsson to her management as a National Marine Sanctuary by NOAA in the 1980's. Specific needs will be:

   —Location of suitable text authors.
   —Compilation of bibliographical and textual data.
   —Determination of suitable publication format.

C. Multimedia material oriented toward reaching the general public to make known the history of the MONITOR and the information generated from recent scientific research.

   —NOAA has available on request a 28 minute, color, sound, 16mm movie "Down to the MONITOR" describing through illustration the famous battle, and through recent filming the discovery of MONITOR artifacts.

   —NOAA and DAH will arrange on request to make available videotapes with sound of the entire 1979 MONITOR expedition jointly sponsored by NOAA, DAH, and Harbor Branch Foundation of Florida.

   —NOAA and DAH provide lectures on the MONITOR sanctuary on request at professional conferences, academic seminars, and other public and scientific programs.

   —NOAA and the Curator of the U.S. Navy will make arrangements on written request to make available for temporary loan artifacts for display from the MONITOR collection.

1. *Study Title:* Produce a professional scientific documentary film of the MONITOR wreck.

Information Needs: To provide the public with an authoritative, entertaining medium with which to communicate the MONITOR's historical and cultural value. Persons knowledgeable in the MONITOR, such as those who have contributed to the text (see Study Title B.3) will be requested to assist NOAA's Public Affairs Office in producing an accurate documentary film.

2. *Study Title:* Develop a traveling MONITOR museum exhibit.

Information Needs: Since the MONITOR is remote and its recovered artifacts few, a traveling museum exhibit would bring the MONITOR to the American people and explain its importance as an irreplaceable cultural resource.

3. *Study Title:* Construct a large scale engineering model of the MONITOR wreck *in situ* with emphasis on structure displacement and bottom topography.

Information Needs: To accurately represent the present arrangement of the MONITOR's remains and to assist investigators in the planning and performance of safe and efficient on-site research activities.

4. *Study Title:* Feasibility study for transmission of a live television picture from the MONITOR Sanctuary to surveillance, research and visitor centers on shore. (Completed: 1981).

Information Needs: Establish feasibility of on-site surveillance and recording of scientific and monitoring observation and explore possibilities to bring the MONITOR to the public via PBC, Cable T.V., etc. (Contracted to: Southwest Research Institute, San Antonio, Texas.)

Regulations

After sanctuary designation in January 1975, to insure public awareness of Federal Laws protecting the MONITOR, NOAA published rules and regulations in the *Federal Register* (Appendix A). These regulations allow transit of surface vessels through the MONITOR Sanctuary, but prohibit activities such as anchoring, salvage and recovery, diving, dredging, detonation of explosives, drilling or coring, cable laying,

trawling, and discharging waste materials. Diving that is consistent with the MONITOR Sanctuary goals may be permissible. However, such activity requires a written permit from NOAA for the purpose of protecting the wreck, assurance of optimum safety procedures, and maintaining a record of the sanctuary's public use. NOAA reserves the rights both to have a representative present during any activity within the sanctuary and to receive a copy of any photographs and/or videotapes that are taken by the permitted researcher (See Appendix B, Research Permits.)

Surveillance and Enforcement

NOAA seeks to insure adequate surveillance and enforcement activities for each designated sanctuary. Such activities are designed on a site-specific basis. In Federal waters, the U.S. Coast Guard (USCG) is the primary enforcement agency and, depending upon the need at any given site, the USCG will enforce sanctuary regulations as a part of their routine surveillance activities depending on budgetary and manpower limitations.

Surveillance and enforcement of regulations for the U.S.S. MONITOR National Marine Sanctuary are carried out by the USCG in cooperation with NOAA and the onsite manager (North Carolina Division of Archives and History). The Coast Guard will report to NOAA any sightings of vessels at the site which appear to be there for purposes not permitted by sanctuary regulations.

Specifically the responsibilities for surveillance and enforcement are as follows:

A. USCG:
- Conducts visual surface and aerial surveillance of the MONITOR National Marine Sanctuary during routine patrols.
- Investigates possible violations of the sanctuary rules and regulations (see Appendix E, Violation Procedure).
- Reports to NOAA suspected or actual violations of the sanctuary rules and regulations.

B. NOAA, On-site Manager, and Commander of the Fifth Coast Guard District, Portsmouth, Virginia.
- Periodically review effectiveness of sanctuary surveillance and enforcement system.

BIBLIOGRAPHY

An asterisk (*) indicates that the publication is available from NOAA.

Bankhead, J.P. 1 January 1863. letter to S.P. Lee, *Official Records of the Union and Confederate Navies in the War of the Rebellion.* (hereinafter cited: O.R.) Washington, 1894-1927, 1, 8:347-8.

Bankhead, J.P. 27 January 1863, letter to G. Welles (MONITOR Papers) United States National Archives, War Records Branch, Navy Section, Naval Records Collection of the Office of Naval Records and Library, Washington, D.C. Record Group 45.

Baxter, James Phinney. *The Introduction of the Ironclad Warship.* Cambridge: Harvard University Press, 1933.

Beachem, C.D., D.A. Meyn, and R.A. Bayles. *Mechanical Properties of Wrought Iron from Hull Plate of U.S.S. MONITOR,* Naval Research Laboratory, Washington, D.C., November 20, 1979, NRL Memorandum Report 4123.

*Brennan, William J. "The MONITOR Marine Sanctuary—An Historic Ship Launches an Important Marine Program." *NOAA Magazine,* April 1975.

Brown, D.R. 10 January 1863, report to S.D. Trenchard, O.R.1, 8:365-8.

Butts, F.B. 1887. The Loss of the MONITOR, published in *Battles and Leaders of the Civil War.* New York.

Carrison, Daniel J. *The Navy from Wood to Steel—1860-1890.* New York: Franklin Watts, 1965.

*Childress, Floyd. "The Lantern." NOAA Magazine, October 1977. pp. 7-9.

*Childress, Floyd, Watts, Gordon P., Jr., Cook, Roger W. and Chester C. Slama. *Preliminary Report, Stereo Photography and Artifact Retrieval, 16 July—2 August 1977. MONITOR Marine Sanctuary,* U.S. National Oceanic and Atmospheric Administration, Office of Coastal Zone Management 1977.

Daly, R.W. (Ed.). 1964, *Aboard the USS MONITOR: 1862* Annapolis.

*D'Angelo, Schoenewaldt Associates (Compiler). "Preliminary Recovery Feasibility Study". U.S.S. MONITOR Technical Report Series, U.S. National Oceanic and Atmospheric Administration, Office of Coastal Zone Management, February 1981.

Eggleston, J.R. "Captain Eggleston's Narrative of the Battle of the Merrimac." *Southern Historical Society Papers,* September 1916.

Ericsson, John. "The Building of the MONITOR." *In Battles and Leaders of the Civil War.* Edited by Robert V. Johnson and Clarence G. Buel. 4 vols. New York: Century, 1887. Vol. 1.

*Gorman, Brian. "U.S.S. MONITOR, The First..." *NOAA Magazine,* January/February 1980.

Greene, Samuel Dana. "An Eyewitness Account": "I Fired the First Gun and Thus Commenced the Great Battle." *American Heritage,* June 1957.

Headley, Phineas Camp. *The Miner Boy and His Monitor; or, the Career and Achievements of John Ericsson, the Engineer.* New York: Appleton, 1865.

Hill, Dina B. (Ed.). "Hull Plate Sample Analysis and Preservation". U.S.S. MONITOR Technical Report Series, U.S. National Oceanic and Atmospheric Administration, Office of Coastal Zone Management, April 1981.

Hoehling, Adolph A. *Thunder at Hampton Roads.* Englewood Cliffs, New Jersey: Prentice Hall, 1976.

"Iron-clad Vessels." *Harper's New Monthly Magazine.* (New York) CXLVIII September, 1862.

Fox, G.V. January 30, 1862, Telegram to J. Ericsson, O.R., 1, 6:538.

Jones, Virgil Carrington. "An Ironclad for Davy Jones." In his *The Civil War at Sea: March 1862—July 1863; The River War.* Vol 2. New York: Holt, Rinehart and Winston, 1961.

Keeler, William Frederick. *Aboard the U.S.S. MONITOR: 1862: The Letters of Acting Paymaster William Frederick Keeler, U.S. Navy to His Wife, Anna.* Edited by Robert W. Daly (Naval Letters Series. V.2.) Annapolis, Maryland: U.S. Naval Institute, 1964.

Lee, S. P. December 24, letter to S.D. Trenchard, O.R., 1, 6:338.

Log of the U.S.S. RHODE ISLAND, 29 December 1862 through 1 January 1863. Record Group 45, National Archives, Washington.

MacBride, R. *Civil War Ironclads.* New York. 1962 McCordock, Robert Stanley. *The Yankee Cheese Box.* Philadelphia: Dorrance, 1938.

Melton, M. 1968. The Confederate Ironclads. New York.

Miller, E.M. *The Ship that Launched the Modern Navy.* Annapolis: Leeward Publishing Company, 1979.

Miller, E.M. "Bound for Hampton Roads." *Civil War Times Illustrated,* Volume XX, Number 4, July 1981, pp. 22-31.

*Muga, Bruce. *Engineering Investigation of the USS MONITOR*. 1982.

National Trust for Historic Preservation in the United States. *The MONITOR—Its Meaning and Future. Papers from a National Conference*. Raleigh, North Carolina. April 2-4, 1978. The Preservation Press, Washington, D.C. 1978.

Newton, John G. "How We Found the MONITOR." *National Geographic*. January 1975, pp. 48-61.

Peterkin, Ernest. "Building a Vehemoth." *Civil War Times Illustrated*. Volume XX, Number 4, July 1981.

Praist, Paul H. "Ships that Changed the War." *U.S. Naval Institute Proceedings*, June 1961, pp. 76-89.

Preston, Robert L. "Did the *Monitor* or *Merrimac* Revolutionize Naval Warfare?" *William and Mary Quarterly*, July 1915, pp. 58-66.

Senate Executive Document 86, 40th Congress, 2nd Session, Washington, 1868.

Shapack, Arnold R. "Oak to Iron-Monitors in the United States Naval History." Master's thesis, University of Maryland, 1973.

*Southwest Research Institute. *A Feasibility Study for Transmission of a Live Television Picture of the USS MONITOR to Visitor Centers Onshore*. 1982.

State of North Carolina, Department of Cultural Resources, Division of Archives and History. *Minutes of Meeting Held at the Smithsonian Concerning the U.S.S. MONITOR*, October 23, 1978.

*Still, William N., Jr. "Archival Sources." U.S.S. MONITOR Technical Report Series, U.S. National Oceanic and Atmospheric Administration, Office of Coastal Zone Management, February 1981.

Still, William N., Jr. "Confederate Naval Strategy: The Ironclad." *Journal of Southern History*, August 1961, pp. 330-343 and Iron Afloat, Auburn, 1971.

Still, William N., Jr. "The Most Cowardly Exhibition", *Civil War Times Illustrated*. Volume XX, Number 4, July 1981, pp. 32-37.

Tise, Larry E. "Searching for the MONITOR." *Civil War Times Illustrated*. Volume XX, Number 4, July 1981, pp. 38-44, 44-45.

Trenchard, S.D. 3 January 1863, report to S.P. Lee. O.R. 1, 8:350-1.

Trenchard, S.D. 10 January 1863, report to J.P. Bankhead. O.R. 1, 8:357-8.

*Tucker, Rockwell G. (Compiler). "Environmental Data." U.S.S. MONITOR Technical Report Series, U.S. National Oceanic and Atmospheric Administration, Office of Coastal Zone Management, February 1981.

*U.S. National Oceanic and Atmospheric Administration. *Final Environmental Impact Statement Summary: Designation of the Submerged Wreckage of the MONITOR as a Marine Sanctuary*, 1974.

*U.S. National Oceanic and Atmospheric Administration. "Investigating the Remains of the U.S.S. MONITOR. A Final Report on the 1979 Site Testing in the MONITOR National Marine Sanctuary." NOAA in cooperation with the North Carolina Department of Cultural Resources, 1981.

*U.S. National Oceanic and Atmospheric Administration. "Operations Manual: MONITOR Marine Sanctuary—A Photogrammatic Survey." NOAA in cooperation with Harbor Branch Foundation, Inc., July 1977.

*U.S. National Oceanic and Atmospheric Administration. "Operations Manual: MONITOR Marine Sanctuary—An Archaeological and Engineering Assessment." NOAA, in cooperation with Harbor Branch Foundation, Inc., and the North Carolina Department of Cultural Resources, August 1979.

Washington, D.C. National Archives. Log of the U.S.S. MONITOR, Record Group 45.

Watters, J. January 1, 1863, report to J.P. Bankhead. O.R., 1, 8:349-50.

*Watts, Gordon P., Jr. *Investigating the Remains of the USS Monitor: A Final Report on 1979 Site Testing in the Monitor National Marine Sanctuary*. 1982. (limited copies available).

Watts, Gordon P., Jr. "The Location and Identification of the Ironclad U.S.S. MONITOR." *The International Journal of Nautical Archaeology and Underwater Exploration*. September 1975, pp. 301-329.

Watts, Gordon P., Jr. and James A. Pleasants, Jr. *U.S.S. MONITOR: A Bibliography*. 1981.

*Watts, Gordon P., Jr. Pleasants, James A., Cook, Roger W., and Morris, Kenneth.

"Preliminary Report: Archaeological and Engineering Expedition MONITOR Marine Sanctuary, August 1-26, 1979." U.S. National Oceanic and Atmospheric Administration, Office of Coastal Zone Management, 1979. Floyd Childress and Sarah Goodnight, ed.

Webber, R.J. 1969, Monitors of the U.S. Navy. Washington.

Welles, G. March 6, 1862. Telegram to H. Paulding. O.R. 1, 6:682

Welles, G. (Compiler). The Original United States Warship "MONITOR" New Haven, Connecticut: Cornelius S. Bushnell National Memorial Association, 1899.

White, William Chapman and Ruth M. White. *Tin Can on a Shingle*. New York: Dutton, 1957.

Worden, John Lorimer. *The MONITOR and the MERRIMAC: Both Sides of the Story Told by Lieut. J.L. Worden, U.S.N. Lieut. Greene, U.S.N. of the MONITOR, and H. Ashton Ramsay, C.S.C., Chief Engineer of the MERRIMAC*. New York: Harper, 1912 APPENDIX B:

*1982 MONITOR National Marine Sanctuary Management Plan. 1982.

*1983 MONITOR National Marine Sanctuary Management Plan. 1983.

APPENDIX A: RULES AND REGULATIONS

MONDAY MAY 19, 1975
WASHINGTON, D.C.

Volume 40 Number 97—*FEDERAL REGISTER*

Part I

DEPARTMENT OF COMMERCE
National Oceanic and Atmospheric Administration

MONITOR MARINE SANCTUARY
Final Regulations

Chapter IX-NATIONAL OCEANIC AND ATMOSPHERIC ADMINISTRATION,
DEPARTMENT OF COMMERCE

PART 924—MONITOR MARINE SANCTUARY

FINAL REGULATIONS

On January 30, 1975, the Secretary of Commerce designated as a marine sanctuary an area of the Atlantic Ocean around and above the submerged wreckage of the Civil War ironclad MONITOR pursuant to the authority of Section 302(a) of the Marine Protection, Research and Sanctuaries Act of 1972 (86 Stat 1052, 1061, hereafter the Act). The sanctuary area (hereafter the Sanctuary) is about 16.10 miles south-southeast of Cape Hatteras (North Carolina) Light.

Section 302(f) of the Act directs the Secretary to issue necessary and reasonable regulations to control any activities permitted within a designated marine sanctuary. This section also provides that no permit, license, or other authorization issued pursuant to any other authority shall be valid unless the Secretary shall certify that the permitted activity is consistent with the purposes of Title III of the Act ("Marine Sanctuaries"); and that it can be carried out within the regulations promulgated under section 302(f).

The authority of the Secretary to administer the provisions of the Act has been delegated to the Administrator, National Oceanic and Atmospheric Administration, U.S. Department of Commerce (hereafter the Administrator, 39 FR 10255, March 19, 1974).

On February 5, 1975, the Administrator published in the *Federal Register* interim regulations applicable to the MONITOR Marine Sanctuary (40 FR 5347), and invited comments on these regulations until March 7, 1975. Comments which have been received have suggested six changes in the regulations as follows:

1. That Section 924.2, the description of the Sanctuary, be somewhat shortened and revised to read:

The Sanctuary consists of a vertical water column in the Atlantic Ocean one mile in diameter extending from the surface to the seabed, the center of which is at 35°00'23" north latitude and 73°24'32" west longitude.

2. That Section 924.3, which prohibits "bottom anchoring" in the Sanctuary, be revised to read:

Anchoring in any manner, stopping, remaining, or drifting without power at any time.

3. That Section 924.3(i), which prohibits the "discharging of waste material" into the waters of the Sanctuary, be revised to read:

Discharging waste material into the water in violation of any Federal statute or regulation.

It was stated that this change was felt to be desirable because of the breadth of the original language, and the difficulty of enforcing a prohibition which could be constructed to extend to routine operational discharges from vessels-such as bilge, sanitary and galley wastes-which discharges would have no adverse impact on the MONITOR.

4. That Section 924.4, which lists penalties for the commission of prohibited acts within the Sanctuary, be revised to read:

Section 303 of the Act authorizes the assessment of a civil penalty of not more than $50,000.00 against any citizen of the United States for each violation of any regulation issued pursuant to Title III of the Act, and further authorizes proceedings in rem against any vessel used in violation of the penalty described above. See also 15 CFR 922 (published at 39 FR 23254 23257. June 27, 1974), for details applicable to any instance of a violation of these regulations.

Essentially this change substitutes "the penalty described above" for "Any such regulations" at the end of the first sentence of the interim regulations; and rephrases the second and third sentences without substantially changing their meaning.

5. That so much of the last part of Section 924.5 as provides that "except that, no permit is required for the conduct of any activity immediately necessary in connection with an air or marine casualty" be revised to read:

> "except that, no permit is required for the conduct of any activity necessary for the protection of life, property or the environment."

The suggested change would appear to add an environmental casualty, such as oil spill, to the air and/or marine casualties already contemplated by the regulation.

6. That Section 924.7, having to do with certification procedures, be revised so as to require any Federal agency which, as of the effective date of the regulations, has authorized any prohibited activity in the Sanctuary, be required to notify the Administrator of that fact in writing. The change was from "activity," as stated in the interim regulations, to "prohibited activity". It was stated that the Secretary's concern should be with any prohibited activity, not with an activity not prohibited.

Except as noted below, and for the reasons there set out, the Administrator has decided to accept these suggested changes, and they have been incorporated into the final regulations. With regard to the suggested changes in Section 924.4 (paragraph 4. above) it is felt that the substitution of "penalty" for "regulations" somewhat misstates the thought involved since the violation in question is of the regulations, not of the penalty. Otherwise, the suggested changes do not alter the meaning of the interim language. Therefore Section 924.4 will be retained in its present form. With regard to the suggested change in Section 924.5 (paragraph 5. above), it is felt that there must be an immediate and urgent need for the activity if it is to be conducted without a permit. Therefore the words "immediately and urgently" will be added before "necessary". At the same time, it is felt that a permit should be required for any activity to be conducted in a sanctuary pertaining to an air or marine casualty already passed, in regard to which there is no need for immediate entry into the sanctuary, such as in relation to salvage or recovery operations. Therefore Section 924.5 (a) (2) has been appropriately modified. Finally the Administrator felt it desirable to provide for the exten-

sion of the various time limits prescribed in Sec 924.3 for good cause shown. This has been done by the addition of a new paragraph (e).

There having been no other comments, and the Administrator being of the view that no additional changes in the regulations are necessary at this time, there are published herewith final regulations pertaining to the MONITOR Marine Sanctuary to become effective May 19, 1975.

15 CFR Part 924 is revised as follows:

Sec.
924.1 Authority.
924.2 Description of the Sanctuary.
924.3 Activities Prohibited Within the Sanctuary.
924.4 Penalties for Commission of Prohibited Acts
924.5 Permitted Activities.
924.6 Permit Procedures and Criteria.
924.7 Certification Procedures.
924.8 Appeals of Administrative Action.

AUTHORITY: Secs. 302(f), 302(g), 303 Marine Protection, Research and Sanctuaries Act of 1972.

924.1 Authority.

The Sanctuary has been designated by the Secretary of Commerce pursuant to the authority of Section 302 (a) of the Act. The following regulations are issued pursuant to the authorities of Sections 302 (f), 302 (g) and 303 of the Act.

924.2 Description of the Sanctuary.

The Sanctuary consists of a vertical water column in the Atlantic Ocean one mile in diameter extending from the surface to the seabed, the center of which is at 35°00'23" north latitude and 75°24'32" west longitude.

924.3 Activities prohibited within the Sanctuary.

Except as may be permitted by the Administrator, no person subject to the jurisdiction of the United States shall conduct, nor cause to be conducted, any of the following activities in the Sanctuary:

(a) anchoring in any manner, stopping, remaining, or drifting without power at any time;

(b) any type of subsurface salvage or recovery operation;

(c) any type of diving whether by an individual or by a submersible;

(d) lowering below the surface of the water any grappling, suction, conveyor, dredging or wrecking device;

(e) detonation below the surface of the water of any explosive or explosive mechanism;

(f) seabed drilling or coring;

(g) lowering, laying, positioning or raising any type of seabed cable or cablelaying device;

(h) trawling; or

(i) discharging waste material into the water in violation of any Federal statute or regulation.

924.4 Penalties for commission of prohibited acts.

Section 303 of the Act authorizes the assessment of a civil penalty of not more than $50,000 for each violation of any regulation issued pursuant to Title III of the Act, and further authorizes a proceeding in rem against any vessel used in violation of any such regulation. Details are set out in Subpart (D) of Part 922 of this Chapter (39 FR 23254, 23257, June 27, 1974). Subpart (D) is applicable to any instance of a violation of these regulations.

924.5 Permitted Activities.

Any person or entity may conduct in the Sanctuary any activity listed in 924.3 of this Part if: (a) such activity is either (1) for the purpose of research related to the MONITOR, or (2) pertains to salvage or recovery operations in connection with an air or marine casualty; and (b) such person or entity is in possession of a valid permit issued by the Administrator authorizing the conduct of such activity; except that no permit is required for the conduct of any activity immediately and urgently necessary for the protection of life, property or the environment.

924.6 Permit Procedures and Criteria.

(a) Any person or entity who wishes to conduct in the Sanctuary an activity for which a permit is authorized by Section 924.5 (hereafter a permitted activity) may apply in writing to the Administrator for a permit to conduct such activity citing this section as the basis for the application. Such application should be made to the Administrator, National Oceanic and Atmospheric Administration, U.S. Department of Commerce, Washington, D.C. 20230. Upon receipt of such application the Administrator shall request and such person or entity shall supply to the Administrator such information and in such form as the Administrator may require to enable him to act upon the application.

(b) In considering whether to grant a permit for the conduct of a permitted activity for the purpose of research related to the MONITOR, the Secretary shall evaluate such matters as (1) the general professional and financial responsibility of the applicant; (2) the appropriateness of the research method(s) envisioned to the purpose(s) of the research; (3) the extent to which the conduct of any permitted activity may diminish the value of the MONITOR as a source of historic, cultural, aesthetic and/or maritime information; (4) the end value of the research envisioned; and (5) such other matters as the Administrator deems appropriate.

(c) In considering whether to grant a permit for the conduct of a permitted activity in the Sanctuary in relation to an air or marine casualty, the Administrator shall consider such matters as (1) the fitness of the applicant to do the work envisioned; (2) the necessity of conducting such activity; (3) the appropriateness of any activity envisioned to the purpose of the entry into the Sanctuary; (4) the extent to which the conduct of any such activity may diminish the value of the MONITOR as a source of historic, cultural, aesthetic and/or maritime information; and (5) such other matters as the Administrator deems appropriate.

(d) In considering any application submitted pursuant to this Section the Administrator may seek and consider the views of any person or entity, within or outside of the Federal Government, as he deems appropriate; except that he shall seek and consider the views of the Advisory Council on Historic Preservation.

(e) The Administrator may, in his discretion grant a permit which has been applied for pursuant to this Section, in whole or in part, and subject to such condition(s) as he deems appropriate except that the Administrator shall attach to any permit granted for research related to the MONITOR the condition that any information and/or artifact(s) obtained in the research shall be made available to the public. The Administrator may observe any activity permitted by this Section and/or may require the submission of one or more reports of the status or progress of such activity.

(f) A permit granted pursuant to this Section is nontransferable.

(g) The Administrator may amend, suspend or revoke a permit granted pursuant to this Section in whole or in part, temporarily or indefinitely if, in his view the permit holder (hereafter the Holder) has acted in violation of the terms of the permit; or the Administrator may do so for other good cause shown. Any such action shall be in writing to the Holder, and shall set forth the reason(s) for the action taken. Any Holder in relation to whom such action has been taken may appeal the action as provided in 924.8 of this Part.

924.7 Certification Procedures.

Any Federal agency which, as of the effective date of these regulations, already has permitted, licensed or otherwise authorized any prohibited activity in the Sanctuary shall notify the Administrator of this fact in writing. The writing shall include a reasonably detailed description of such activity, the person(s) involved, the beginning and ending dates of such permission the reason(s) and purpose(s) for same and a description of the total area affected. The Administrator shall then decide whether the continuation of the permitted activity, in whole or in part, or subject to such condition(s) as he may deem appropriate is consistent with the purposes of Title III of the Act and can be carried out within these regulations. He shall inform the Federal agency of his decision in these regards and the reason(s) therefore, in writing. The decision of the Secretary made pursuant to this Section shall be final action for the purpose of the Administrative Procedure Act.

924.8 Appeals of Administrative Action.

(a) In any instance in which the Administrator, as regards a permit authorized by, or issued pursuant to, this Part: (1) denies a permit (2) issues a permit embodying less authority than was requested; (3) conditions a permit in a manner unacceptable to the applicant; or (4) amends, suspends, or revokes a permit for a reason other than the violation of regulations issued under this Part, the applicant or the permit holder, as the case may be (hereafter the Appellant), may appeal the Administrator's action to the Secretary. In order to be considered by the Secretary, such appeal shall be in writing, shall state the action(s) appealed and the reason(s) therefore; and shall be submitted within 30 days of the action(s) by the Administrator to which the appeal is directed. The Appellant may request a hearing on the appeal.

(b) Upon receipt of an appeal authorized by this Section, the Secretary may request, and if he does, the Appellant shall provide such additional information and in such form as the Secretary may request in order to enable him to act upon the appeal. If the Appellant has not requested a hearing the Secretary shall decide the appeal upon (1) the basis of the criteria set out in Section 924.6(b) or Section 924.6(c) of this part, as appropriate (2) information relative to the application on file in NOAA (3) information provided by the Appellant, and (4) such other considerations as he deems appropriate. He shall notify the Appellant of his decision, and the reason(s) therefore in writing within 30 days of the date of his receipt of the appeal.

(c) If the Appellant has requested a hearing the Secretary shall grant an informal hearing before a Hearing Officer designated for that purpose by the Secretary after first giving notice of the time, place, and subject matter of the hearing in the FEDERAL REGISTER. Such hearing shall be held no later than 30 days following the Secretary's receipt of the appeal. The Appellant and any interested person may appear personally or by counsel at the hearing, present evidence, cross-examine witnesses, offer argument and file a brief. Within 30 days of the last day of the hearing, the Hearing Officer shall recommend in writing a decision to the Secretary based upon the considerations outlined in paragraph (b) of this Section and based upon the record made at the hearing.

(d) The Secretary may adopt the Hearing Officer's recommended decision in whole or in part, or may reject or modify it. In any event the Secretary shall notify the Appellant of his decision and the reason(s) therefore, in writing within 15 days of his receipt of the recommended decision of the Hearing Officer. The Secretary's action, whether without or after a hearing as the case may be, shall constitute final action for the purposes of the Administrative Procedure Act.

(e) Any time limit prescribed in this Section may be extended by the Secretary for good cause, either upon the Secretary's own motion and upon written notification to an Appellant stating the reason(s) therefore, or upon the written request of an Appellant to the Secretary stating the reason(s) therefore, except that no time limit may be extended more than 30 days.

R. L. CARNAHAN
Acting Assistant Administrator for Administration
FR Doc. 75-13009 Filed 5-16-75;8:45am

APPENDIX B: RESEARCH PERMITS

Scientific and archaeological research is encouraged in the MONITOR National Marine Sanctuary. Written application for research permits should be submitted to:

Assistant Administrator
National Ocean Service, NOAA
Attn: Sanctuary Program Division
3300 Whitehaven Street, N.W.
Washington, DC 20235

The permits are issued in accordance with Title III of the Marine Protection, Research and Sanctuaries Act of 1972 (86 Stat. 1051; 16 USC 1431-1434) and regulations under 15 CFR Parts 922, 924.

Research proposals should be organized to include a table of contents, abstract, bibliography, the background (what events led to this proposal), research design and description, a description of planned data management techniques, and qualifications of research personnel. The proposal also must include a description of the expected impact of the proposed research on site, the time required for the research (including duration of in-the-field time), and expected date of submission of the draft and final reports. If the research includes the recovery of artifacts, a detailed plan must be submitted which includes analysis, conservation,

funding commitments, and a statement of where field and lab records will be curated.

NOAA has established a system by which proposals for research within the MONITOR National Marine Sanctuary can be reviewed and evaluated by members of the scientific community and appropriate Federal agencies before NOAA decides to issue a permit. A Memorandum of Agreement assigns to the State of North Carolina the responsibility for administering the review process : research proposals as well as for assisting interested scientists in the development of research proposals.

For specific details on the review procedure, refer to the MOA in Appendix D. Anyone needing assistance in preparing research proposals can contact the North Carolina Division of Archives and History. Initial inquiries should be made at least twelve weeks before the January 1, deadline. Address inquiries to:

MONITOR Research Review Coordinator
State of North Carolina
Department of Cultural Resources
Division of Archives and History
109 East Jones Street
Raleigh, NC 27611
(919) 733-7305 or (919) 458-9042

APPENDIX C: POLICY FOR MANAGEMENT OF MONITOR COLLECTIONS

INTRODUCTION

NOAA has responsibility for managing and preserving recovered collections generated from the research at the MONITOR National Marine Sanctuary. NOAA's other responsibility is to make collections available for research and exhibits.

In executing these responsibilities, NOAA has developed a system for collections management with the Curator for the Navy. A joint NOAA/Navy Memorandum of Understanding (MOU) designates the Department of the Navy to provide the curatorial services required for the proper management and control of artifacts recovered from the MONITOR National Marine Sanctuary. Included in these requirements is a continuous register of the MONITOR collections and catalogue descriptions, photographs of all artifacts, and compilation of conservation information. The management of exhibitions and storage of artifacts are also the responsibility of the Curator for the Navy. With NOAA, the Navy will review applications for the loan of artifacts and will, with NOAA's concurrence, arrange for the loan of objects for exhibition.

The artifacts registration procedure will be the responsibility of the Curator for the Navy. After items recovered from the MONITOR have been duly iden-

tified, measured, weighed (if deemed necessary), photographed and properly preserved under NOAA's supervision, the artifacts and all associated documentation will be transferred to the Curator for the Navy. On receipt of materials and related data in good condition, the Curator will assume responsibility for these properties. The Curator will enter the information into the Navy's computerized registration system and will assign an accession number to each item which will henceforth serve as a control number. The record on each individual artifact will fully identify that object and include its present location and conditions as of the last report.

1. OUTLINE OF MANAGEMENT PROCEDURE

Research permit requirements assure that planning for collections management is introduced in the proposal phase and is fully developed in the research design with funding commitments. Parties interested in seeking a permit for research involving the retrieval of artifacts must provide in the initial proposal a description of a plan for conservation which minimizes deterioration and insures preservation of the artifacts collected. Analysis should include at a minimum: Photography and cataloging of the artifacts, and a statement of curatorial responsibilities for the original field and lab records. A description of the preservation process to be applied to recovered objects must also be provided. The proposal is then examined by the Federal Review Committee, the on-site manager, and their Advisory Task Force. If approved, NOAA will issue the research permit.

After the above requirements are met to NOAA's satisfaction, the objects and pertinent records are to be transferred to the Curator for the Navy. If the principal investigator can provide appropriate environmentally controlled, secure, and accessible facilities, he/she may retain, with NOAA's approval, the collections on a temporary loan and the transfer of properties to the Curator for the Navy will proceed on paper only. A formal loan agreement would then be executed.

2. ELIGIBILITY FOR REGISTRATION

The principal investigator (the "permittee" for research) will be responsible for the cost of transferring recovered objects to the Curator for the Navy after the following conditions of acceptance for registration have been met:

a. Proper conservation treatment is completed and records describing the techniques, chemical processes, and specific long-term maintenance problems (such as the degradation potential of protective coatings) are provided,

b. The artifacts are cataloged and photographed,

c. Copies of pertinent documents supporting the identification of the objects that will be useful in carrying out the curatorial function are provided, e.g., research proposal, operations manual, field and analytical records, and published works and manuscript sources, among others, and

d. Preferably, recovered artifacts are to be delivered to the Curator for the Navy by the permittee at the Washington Navy Yard, in Washington, D.C. Items small enough to be forwarded through the Postal Service by registered mail shall be addressed as follows:

Curator for the Navy
Naval Historical Center
Washington Navy Yard
Washington, DC 20374

Large crated items are to be shipped as follows:

Receiving Officer
Supply and Fiscal Department
Building 176
Washington Navy Yard
Washington, DC 20374

The Curator for the Navy can be reached at (202) 433-2220/2318.

3. REGISTRATION

The Curator for the Navy will be responsible for maintaining registration records for MONITOR

artifacts recovered from the MONITOR National Marine Sanctuary. In so doing, the Curator will:

a. Preserve the integrity of the archaeologist's collecting strategies and analytical procedures within the registration process.

b. Develop a cross index system to relate to the permittee's initial field or lab assessing process of all properties recovered from the MONITOR during research.

c. An in-house computerized accessioning system capability allows input and recall of data from the Curator's own office space. This added facility renders the present system all the more responsive to inquiries on the MONITOR objects.

4. STORAGE AND EXHIBITION

The Curator for the Navy will be responsible to NOAA for maintaining the MONITOR collection by providing stable environmental control for artifacts in Navy custody and assuring NOAA that such artifacts are secure while in storage. The Curator will submit an annual report to NOAA covering all items in the collection, those in storage, on exhibit, on loan and those added to the collection during the current calendar year. This report will, in turn, require the Curator to inspect personally all objects in the collection annually. The Curator will require, on the anniversary date of the loan, written reports with accompanying photographs of all objects from the borrowers at sites where Curator visitation is not feasible.

Exhibitions will be encouraged. However, their design, construction, and associated costs will be the responsibility of the requesting organization. Neither NOAA nor the Curator for the Navy is staffed or funded to provide such services. Prior to their execution proposed exhibit designs and plans are to be submitted by eligible organizations for review by both NOAA and the Curator for the Navy. On receipt of approval, organizations can proceed with their plans as submitted or modified.

5. LOANS

Institutions interested in the loan of artifacts should make a written request to NOAA. NOAA, with the assistance of the Navy, will review the applications and, with NOAA's approval, the Navy will arrange for the loan transaction.

As part of the requirement for obtaining MONITOR artifacts for exhibition, each requesting organization will have to provide NOAA with certain data. For this reason, a form has been developed that poses questions concerning provisions for environmental controls, security, insurance, personnel and funding. This form will be sent to eligible requestors on receipt of their initial inquiry.

MONITOR artifacts can be loaned to educational institutions of higher learning, research organizations, museums, Federal and State agencies and incorporated municipalities that meet the following minimal criteria:

a. Facilities to house artifacts must include environmental control; security; insurance; and when the loan is for exhibit purposes, the facilities must also have museum trained personnel and handicapped persons' accommodations. On application, a Facility Report form will be sent to each organization interested in obtaining MONITOR artifacts.

b. Funding must be available for transporting the materials from the present location to the desired site and return and for preparing a suitable exhibit.

c. A loan agreement must be executed for materials that will be placed with eligible organizations for a maximum of two years. Accompanying the loan agreement will be a report on the condition of the objects as they leave the custody of the Curator for the Navy. At the end of one year, the borrower will submit an updated report on the present condition of the objects; the Curator will prepare a report on the objects' condition at the time of their return.

6. DEACCESSIONING

If deaccessioning becomes necessary, the decision to do so will be evaluated by the Curator for the Navy, the onsite manager, and the Technical Advisory Committee who then pass on their recommendations to NOAA for final decision. "Deaccession" is the permanent transfer of custody for an object to another institution or disposal by means of destruction, in which case, the object may not under any circumstance become part of a personal curation.

7. AVAILABILITY OF COLLECTION

All collections and records made under the provisions of a NOAA permit must be available for research and public education without charge and upon reasonable notice.

APPENDIX D: MEMORANDUM OF AGREEMENT

1983 MEMORANDUM OF AGREEMENT between the National Oceanic and Atmospheric Administration and the North Carolina Division of Archives and History for Management of the MONITOR National Marine Sanctuary.

I. BACKGROUND

The MONITOR Marine Sanctuary was created pursuant to the Title III of the Marine Protection, Research, and Sanctuaries Act of 1972, Public Law 92-532, on January 30, 1975. Since that time, the Director of the Division of Archives and History, hereinafter referred to as Director, has been designated on-site manager of the sanctuary to assist the Marine Sanctuary Projects Manager (SPM) of the National Oceanic and Atmospheric Administration (NOAA) with the planning and implementation of specific management-related research activities and in assisting investigators in the preparation of proposals to conduct research in the sanctuary. The Director, as Review Coordinator, has been responsible for conducting an annual review of all proposed research projects and coordinating the activities of the Technical Advisory Committee. All assistance by the Director has to date been through an annually renewable Memorandum of Agreement (MOA).

1. At the time of this agreement, NOAA's Marine Sanctuary Projects Manager is:
   Dr. Richard J. Podgorny
   Sanctuary Projects Manager

Sanctuary Programs Division
National Oceanic and Atmospheric
  Administration
3300 Whitehaven Street, N.W.
Washington, DC 20235

2. At the time of this agreement, the Director, Division of Archives and History/Review Coordinator, Dr. William S. Price, Jr., has delegated the responsibilities outlined in this MOA to:
   Dr. John J. Little
   Administrator/Deputy State Historic
     Preservation Officer
   Division of Archives and History
   North Carolina Department of Cultural
     Resources
   109 East Jones Street
   Raleigh, NC 27611

3. The individual responsible for providing technical assistance for research operations conducted at the site and technical support in monitoring permitted research in the sanctuary is entitled Operations Coordinator. At the time of this agreement, the Operations Coordinator is:
   Mr. Richard W. Lawrence, Head
   Underwater Archaeology Unit
   Division of Archives and History
   P.O. Box 58
   Kure Beach, NC 28449

4. The individual responsible for managing all activities related to the State's involvement with the

MONITOR National Marine Sanctuary and serving as liaison between the State on-site sanctuary projects manager (Director) and the Federal Marine Sanctuary Projects Manager (SPM) is entitled Sanctuary Coordinator. At the time of this agreement the Sanctuary Coordinator is:

> Ms. Diana M. Lange, MONITOR Sanctuary
> Coordinator
> Underwater Archaeology Unit
> Division of Archives and History
> P.O. Box 58
> Kure Beach, NC 28449

II. PROPOSAL

Because the MONITOR-related activities and responsibilities of the Division of Archives and History have greatly increased since the creation of the sanctuary, the Director proposes to expand the current MEMORANDUM OF AGREEMENT to reflect the growth and diversity of those responsibilities. (Contact NOAA's Marine Sanctuary Programs Division for copies of the original 1975 Memorandum of Agreement).

The Director and other personnel of the Division of Archives and History will continue to assist in all phases of management-related activities, to coordinate the review of research proposals. coordinate and participate in meetings as necessary, supervise contractual projects, and conduct other activities that are required to facilitate the effective management of the MONITOR National Marine Sanctuary.

III. STATE OF NORTH CAROLINA AND DIRECTOR, DIVISION OF ARCHIVES AND HISTORY'S RESPONSIBILITIES

1. The Director, Division of Archives and History will plan and undertake specific management related research activities as mutually agreed upon with NOAA which will include (1) providing technical assistance in engineering, marine archaeology and conservation, (2) provide technical support in monitoring permitted research in the sanctuary, (3) administering the review process for proposals to conduct research in the sanctuary and (4) publishing reports and educational materials prepared by the North Carolina Division of Archives and History or by contract with other individuals.

2. The Director will organize a yearly meeting of the Technical Advisory Committee and appropriate staff personnel from NOAA and the Division of Archives and History to discuss current research proposals and to review the management goals and objectives outlined in the MONITOR National Marine Sanctuary Management Plan.

3. The Director will apprise and seek appropriate guidance from NOAA's Sanctuary Projects Manager (SPM) as he assists investigators in the preparation of each proposal for research in the sanctuary, collect and coordinate all completed proposals and conduct an annual review of all such proposals received prior to November 1st of each year according to the following schedule:

a. By November 10th the Director will mail a copy of each proposal received to NOAA's SPM and to every member of the Federal Review Committee, Technical Advisory Committee, and to any technical experts the Director selects, or a memo to NOAA indicating no proposals were received.

b. Each reviewer will be given thirty days to review all proposals and submit a recommendation for each proposal accepting it, conditionally accepting it or rejecting it. The Director will insure that all recommendations are received no later than December 15th (and will avoid further use of any technical expert who fails to respond in a timely manner).

c. By January 1st, the Director will forward a recommended decision on each proposal to NOAA's SPM accepting it, rejecting it, or accepting it with conditions. Such decisions shall be supported by appropriate documentation, including copies of all comments and recommendations. Where comments and recommendations are received by December 15th from individuals, agencies or sources other than those specifically solicited in accordance with paragraph (a), the Director shall consider these in making a recommended decision and include them in documentation. Such comments received after December 15th will be forwarded directly to NOAA's SPM.

d. Where review indicates that a modified proposal would be given additional consideration, the Director will contact the applicant and outline the changes determined desirable. The Director shall inform NOAA's SPM of the changes suggested and the time within which he anticipates being able to make a decision on a modified proposal.

4. In cases where previously approved proposals require alteration or where new proposals are received which demonstrate that scheduling immediate review will permit investigators to take advantage of a significant opportunity the Director may initiate the review process at any time during the calendar year. In such cases, the reviewers will normally be given thirty days to review the proposals and the Director will endeavor to coordinate the review in a period of time shorter than this total 45 day period.

5. Where it is clearly evident that a proposed research project represents no threat to the archaeological or historical integrity of the site the Director may, following consultation with at least two recognized authorities with experience in the discipline involving the proposed work, prepare a written report of this finding and recommend to NOAA's SPM that a permit be granted. Where it is determined that there is potential for adverse impact, the proposal will be routed through the normal review process channels.

6. Each application for a research permit in the sanctuary will be evaluated in terms of how the proposed research is related to the sanctuary's preservation, research and education goals. The significance of the research must be examined in terms of the project's contribution to these goals. Each proposal will be considered in light of the potential impact of the proposed work on the archaeological and historical integrity of the MONITOR site. Reviewers will also be asked to evaluate each proposal in terms of their ability to achieve the established objectives of the proposal. Proposal methodology and techniques will be evaluated to determine if data collection and evaluation systems insure the greatest return of information. Equipment used in the research will be evaluated to determine if it is the most appro-

priate available to accomplish the tasks involved and the plan for conservation of any artifacts collected will be evaluated to determine if it is sufficient to minimize deterioration and to insure preservation of artifacts.

7. Governmental agencies or other groups indicating an interest in reviewing proposals will receive copies of all proposals only by submitting a written request to NOAA's SPM.

8. When a decision to grant a permit has been reached the Director will notify the Advisory Council on Historic Preservation of the pending action and will submit the proper documentation to the Council for their review and comment according to the requirements of Section 106, National Historic Preservation Act of 1966. The Commander of the Fifth U.S. Coast Guard District will be notified of any permits issued for activity in the MONITOR National Marine Sanctuary.

IV. NOAA INVOLVEMENT

As part of the joint nature of this effort, NOAA will continue to provide management funds, technical assistance and guidance in matters related to the management of the MONITOR National Marine Sanctuary which require the participation of the Director and North Carolina's Division of Archives and History.

APPENDIX E: VIOLATION PROCEDURE

Violators are subject to civil penalties of up to $50,000 under Public Law 92-532. They will be notified of the alleged violation at the scene by the issuance of a Coast Guard Enforcement Action Report (EAR) CG-520, Offense Investigation Report: (OIR) CG-5202; and Offense Investigation Report Supplement (OIR-SUP): CG-5202-A. Evidentiary materials found in the possession of the violator (i.e., artifacts, concretions, etc.) will be seized by Coast Guard personnel and statements taken. No further action against the violator will normally be taken at this time. Copies of the Enforcement Action or the Offense Investigation Report are distributed as the format indicates. Statements of evidentiary materials are transferred with the copy of the Report of Boarding to the NOAA Office of Gen-

eral Counsel which evaluates all relevant information for sufficiency of evidence and severity of the offense. If appropriate, the NOAA Office of General Counsel draws a notice of violation specifying the precise violation involved and the proposed penalty and sends it to the violator for appropriate action.

If the need arises, U.S. vessels and their operators are subject to seizure by the Coast Guard under the combining authority of 14 USC 89 and 16 USC 1433 (c). If a contempt of court is involved (Sec 16 USC 1433 (d)), the operator would be subject to arrest by the Coast Guard for disobedience of the restraining order. Violations of foreign vessels will be reported to the U.S. Department of State.

APPENDIX F: SANCTUARY DESIGNATION

WHEREAS Title III of the Marine Protection, Research and Sanctuaries Act of 1972, Public Law 92-532, authorized the Secretary of Commerce, with approval of the President of the United States, to designate Marine Sanctuaries; and,

WHEREAS the wreckage of the U.S.S. MONITOR has recently been identified; and,

WHEREAS it is the concensus of concerned organizations and individuals that the wreckage should be protected for its historic, cultural, and technological values; and,

WHEREAS the vessel has been placed on the National Register of Historic Places.

I, THEREFORE, designate the site of the U.S.S. MONITOR to be THE MONITOR MARINE SANCTUARY the area of which is to encompass a vertical section of the water column from the surface to the seabed and extending horizontally one mile in diameter from a center point located at 35°00'23" North Latitude and 75°24'32" West Longitude; and hereby affirm that the regulations promulgated according to the aforementioned authority will provide the necessary protection of law to preserve the esthetic values of this Historic Place.

January 30, 1975

Signature
Frederick B. Dent
Secretary of Commerce

APPENDIX G: SUMMARY OF EXPEDITIONS TO THE MONITOR SITE FOLLOWING ITS INITIAL LOCATION AND IDENTIFICATION

ALCOA SEAPROBE: April 1-7, 1974

Sponsoring Agencies: United States Navy, National Geographic.

Participants: United States Navy, National Geographic, Duke University, North Carolina Division of Archives and History, Massachusetts Institute of Technology.

Purpose: To obtain a complete photographic and television tape record of the wreck, and to collect specific samples of the remains for laboratory analysis.

Description of Work: Although foul weather prevented recovery of the desired samples, SEAPROBE's dynamic positioning and precision photographic systems made it possible to collect more than 1400 high quality photographs of the entire wreck. Several additional hours of television tape records were also made during the photographing process.

Conclusions: Analysis of this data has confirmed the identification of the wreck as that of the MONITOR, and has provided much previously unavailable data about the forward portion of the wreck. Photographs and television tapes of the bow area clearly show the distinct overlapping armor platform forward of the lower hull and the unique circular anchor well. Selected photographs from the collection were used by the Naval Intelligence Support Center to prepare a complete photomosaic of the wreck.

R/V EASTWARD: May, 1974

Sponsoring Agencies: Duke University, University of Delaware.

Participants: Duke University, University of Delaware.

Purpose: To recover bottom samples from the MONITOR site.

Description of Work: While returning from a geophysical survey of the Delaware coast, the EASTWARD was allotted 4 hours to work at the MONITOR site. Twenty five minutes were spent dragging a dredge through the sand in the vicinity of the wreck. Samples recovered include a decklight cover 10 inches in diameter as well as several small ferrous concretions.

Conclusions: While the extent of volumetric corrosion and accumulation of calcareous deposits on the deck light cover, identified as being a type used on the MONITOR, was determined during cleaning, no systematic analysis of the remaining artifacts has been reported.

CGC CHILULA: August 12-16, 1974

Sponsoring Agency: United States Coast Guard.

Participants: United States Coast Guard, Massachusetts Institute of Technology, National Oceanic and Atmospheric Administration, North Carolina Division of Archives and History, United States Navy.

41

Purpose: To determine whether existing portable underwater search equipment provided by the Coast Guard Research and Development Center could be successfully used by Coast Guard ships and boats to locate an underwater target. To utilize an underwater camera strobe system from Massachusetts Institute of Technology and the SNOOPY television/propulsion system from the United States Navy to inspect the wreck of the MONITOR. To recover the camera system lost at the MONITOR site during the August, 1973 expedition and recover further samples from the site.

Description of Work: Due to Federal restrictions prohibiting bottom disturbing activities at the site and the heavy sea state encountered, no recovery or remote camera work was conducted at the site. However, sidescan sonar contact was made with the wreck.

Conclusions: Although no information concerning the MONITOR was gathered during this expedition, the experience proved useful in developing the various search and photographic systems.

R/V BEVERIDGE: August 19-22 and 26-28, 1974

Sponsoring Agency: Duke University.

Participants: Duke University, Massachusetts Institute of Technology.

Purpose: To observe the wreck of the MONITOR with underwater television, retrieve the camera system lost during the August, 1973 expedition, and take horizontal photographs with a new underwater camera strobe system.

Description of Work: The wreck was located using sidescan sonar but due to Federal restrictions no recovery operations were conducted. However, observations were made of the wreck using the underwater television system. For a variety of logistical reasons the underwater camera/strobe system was not used.

Conclusions: Due to the limited amount of data gained on this expedition no conclusions have been published.

R/V EASTWARD: June 9-10 and June 16, 1976

Sponsoring Agencies: National Science Foundation Grant to the Cooperative Oceanographic Program of Duke University Marine Laboratory.

Participants: MONITOR Research and Recovery Foundation, University of Delaware.

Purpose: To obtain data concerning the magnetic field and subbottom acoustic reflectors in the MONITOR National Marine Sanctuary, in conjunction with a geophysical survey of the Delaware continental shelf.

Description of Work: A total of eight crossings of the wreck were made using a Varian proton precession magnetometer during the two periods of research. Acoustic reflection measurements of the wreck site were made utilizing an Edo-western subbottom profiler with a hull mounted 3.5 kHz transducer.

Conclusions: From the magnetic data collected, researchers were able to isolate certain magnetic characteristics of the MONITOR and their effect on the regional magnetic field. It was also concluded that no fragments of ferrous metal larger than 3m on a side exist further than 100m from the wreck. The acoustic data indicated the general direction of slope of the subbottom reflectors in the area, and the MONITOR's relative position to these reflectors.

R/V CAPE HENLOPEN: April 4-8, 1977

Sponsoring Agencies: Exxon Education Foundation, University of Delaware.

Participants: MONITOR Research and Recovery Foundation, National Oceanic and Atmospheric Administration, University of Delaware.

Purpose: To obtain measurements of the near bottom currents, to take coring samples of the sediments beneath the MONITOR wreck, and to conduct horizontal television observations of the wreck.

Description of Work: A Braincon current meter was installed just outside of the MONITOR National Marine Sanctuary to measure the near bottom currents during the period of the expedition. An 18 foot core, was taken southeast of the remains of the MONITOR using a standard 6m Ewing type piston core. Finally, a television camera was lowered to the site enabling a horizontal view of the forward section of the wreck.

Conclusions: From this work the researchers were able to make a number of observations concerning the strength and direction of the near bottom currents in the MONITOR National Marine Sanctuary, the type and condition of the sediments beneath the wreck and what effect these factors will have in future work and recovery operations at the site. In addition, the television cameras provided further information on the structure and condition of the wreck.

R/V JOHNSON and R/V SEA DIVER: July 17—August 2, 1977

Sponsoring Agencies: Harbor Branch Foundation, National Oceanic and Atmospheric Administration.

Participants: Harbor Branch Foundation, National Oceanic and Atmospheric Administration, North Carolina Division of Archives and History, United States Navy.

Purpose: To conduct a photogrammetric survey of the MONITOR and the controlled recovery of material from the MONITOR site.

Description of Work. Preliminary work was carried out using sidescan sonar on the wreck and then searching the surrounding area with this sonar one half mile in all directions to detect any protrusions from the bottom. No such protrusions were found. A remote controlled vehicle, CORD, equipped with a television camera, was sent to the wreck of the MONITOR and closed circuit television pictures were transmitted to the surface vessels. Visibility was quite good, in excess of 100 feet, and the CORD system allowed complete scanning of the wreck from bow to stern. The photogrammetric survey was conducted using two submersibles, JOHNSON-SEA-LINK I, and JOHNSON-SEA-LINK II, and divers who were transported to and from the site in the submersibles. A total of three passes were made over the wreck for the horizontal and oblique stereo photography. Two of these passes were made with black and white film and one with color film. The final operation involved the recovery of an iron hull plate which had been disturbed when a camera system had fouled the wreck during the August, 1973 expedition. The location of this plate had been well documented during previous expeditions as well as during the photogrammetric survey of the wreck. The camera system which fouled the plate and was subsequently lost was also recovered at this time. In addition, a brass signal lantern that had been discovered lying 40 feet north of the turret on the sea floor was recovered to prevent its loss or destruction at the site.

Conclusions: The detailed investigation of the closed circuit television and photogrammetric data coupled with the analysis of the hull plate and brass lantern will greatly add to what is already known concerning the extent and structural integrity of the remains of the MONITOR. From this information it will be possible to more reasonably assess the direction of future work at the site, particularly in planning for any further recovery and preservation of material from the site. This expedition also allowed the first on-site inspection of the wreck by divers and the crews of the submersibles. Their observations have provided insight into the structure and condition of the MONITOR's armor belt, turret, deck, and machinery that was not possible before with the use of remote camera systems.

R V CALYPSO: June 9-14, 1979

Sponsoring Agency: Cousteau Society.

Participants: Cousteau Society.

Purpose: To photograph the MONITOR with movie film to be used as a segment in a one-hour television special on "Historical Wrecks."

Description of Work: Divers using standard SCUBA equipment descended 210 feet to the wreck staying ten minutes at that depth and then ascending at given rates and decompressing for approximately 45 minutes at 30, 20 and 10 feet. Two buoys were positioned near the wreck: one buoy, (B1), 80 meters south of the wreck and another, (B2), 100 meters north. Two film crews, of 4 divers each, moved over the wreck, drifting with the prevailing current from buoy to buoy, filming as they passed. Appproximately 12 minutes of film were exposed, however, film quality was somewhat impaired by poor visibility and low light level.

Conclusions: The methods used by the Cousteau Society were novel in several respects: Use of SCUBA equipment with air as a breathing medium, deployment of eight divers at one time, in water decompression of divers and use of satellite navigation system and radar for positioning. These procedures could have been accomplished only by a team with as much experience as Cousteau's divers. Photographic coverage of the wreck provided additional information on the condition of the wreck as well as environmental conditions at the site.

R/V JOHNSON: August 1-26, 1979

Sponsoring Agencies: National Oceanic and Atmospheric Administration, North Carolina Division of Archives and History, Harbor Branch Foundation, Inc.

Participants: National Oceanic and Atmospheric Administration, North Carolina Division of Archives and History, Harbor Branch Foundation, Inc.

Purpose: To establish permanent reference points adjacent to the wreck, test the structural components of the MONITOR, conduct a test excavation in the forward portion of the wreck within the hull, and undertake a general reconnaissance of the site by diver observations and hand-held photography.

Description of Work: Three underwater archaeologists, supported by a team of 20 technicians, divers, and crew members, conducted 49 dives; during 36 of which the divers left the submersible, JOHNSON-SEA-LINK I, for a working dive. Breathing a gas mixture of 12 percent oxygen and 88 percent helium, the divers spent, per dive, approximately 60 minutes on the bottom and about four and one-half hours in decompression upon return to the support vessel R V JOHNSON. From the excavations, the divers recovered 106 objects of historic and scientific significance representing a broad range of materials including brass, iron, leather, glass, and ceramics. The artifacts have undergone conservation analysis and will be part of a future exhibit on the MONITOR.

Conclusions: Data generated by the research project afforded valuable insight into the archaeological and engineering problems presented by this and other deepwater archaeological sites. This information has significantly broadened the knowledge upon which sanctuary management decisions will be made.

Acknowledgments:
    Special thanks to Ms. Barbara L. Brooks, MONITOR Sanctuary Secretary, North Carolina Division of Archives and History, Kure Beach, N.C., and Ms. Lois Mills, Clerk/typist, NOAA's Sanctuary Programs Division, Washington, D.C. for their invaluable assistance in preparing this document for publication.